Stanley Baxter

The Parliamo Glasgow Omnibus

Stanley Baxter

The
Parliamo Glasgow
Omnibus

Birlinn

This edition published in 2002 by
Birlinn Limited
West Newington House
10 Newington Road
Edinburgh
EH9 1QS

www.birlinn.co.uk

Reprinted 2003, 2005

First published in two volumes by Paul Harris Publishing

ISBN 1 874744 00 9

British Library Cataloguing-in-Publication Data
A Catalogue record for this book is available
from the British Library

Printed and Bound by Cox & Wyman Ltd, Reading, Berkshire

Contents

Foreword

At last! All my "Parliamo Glasgows" within one volume. I hope it will be a bumper fun book for all the family of Scots both at home and abroad who treasure the Glasgow "patter".

I originally came up with the idea of treating broad Glasgow speech as a foreign language and translating it into English in the early fifties when I was still a member of the Citizens' Theatre Company. It was for a radio show and I thought it would be fun to have an elderly Oxbridge-type professor of anthropology visit the Glasgow "tribe" and recount his experiences. This went down so well with the radio audience that I repeated it on stage in the "Five-Past Eight" shows.

After doing two or three "Professors" on T.V. I said to the man who had written them "can we get away from a 'talking head' and open up this idea for television?" Alex Mitchell – for it was he – came up with the idea of spoofing "Parliamo Italiano" – an adult education series that was then current. We followed its format precisely and Scotland simply fell in love with the item.

It led not only to lots more being written for me by Alex – but to many imitators all over the place. Dundee came up with its

Dundonian version – and even Australia with "Let's Talk Strine".

But there was only one Alex Mitchell and his death two years ago brought "Parliamo Glasgow" to an end. So this bumper edition is a keepsake of all the ones he wrote and I performed with such relish.

Parliamo Glasgow

At the Discotheque

Lecturer: In certain discotheques in Glasgow the more obscure words and phrases used by the native dancers may not be understood by non-Glasgwegian patrons. As one enters such an establishment one may hear the word –
MASHUR
This can form a greeting when the letter "O" is put in front of it and added to it is the word –
SELSOTIZ
And there is our greeting –
OMASHURSELSOTIZ
In English – "Oh my, it is yourself, so it is". Again –
MASHUR
is often employed by a young man in a disco when he first catches sight of a prepossessing damsel. This time, however, it is preceded by three words –
AWANNI
GERRAHODDA and RATS
and so we have the fervent declaration –
AWANNI GERRAHODDA RATS MASHUR
He thus indicates that he wishes to take hold of the young lady and dance with her ...

Of course, the word undergoes a subtle change of meaning when used by a gentleman who finds dancing a

3

rather warm proceeding. He will then exclaim –

MASHUR

This is quickly followed by the words –

TAIL
STIKKINTI
MABAHOOKI

which gives us the dramatic disclosure –

MASHURTAIL STIKKINTIMABAHOOKI

Another interesting word heard in the discotheque is

JIWANNI

To a young lady a gentleman will make the request –

JIWANNI DANCE?

Should she find that he is over-anxious to ply her with refreshments she will regard him with suspicion and inquire –

JIWANNI GETMIBEVVID?
JIWANNI

in certain circumstances changes to –

JIWANNA

used generally in conjunction with the word –

BELTOANRAMOOTH

A female dancer who is sneered at by another maiden may threaten her detractor with facial damage. And so she utters the sinister sentence –

JIWANNABELTOANRAMOOTH?

When a young lady is invited to a gentleman's flat for "coffee or something" she knows intuitively what the "something" is. Thereupon she will reply in ringing tones –

KAMMACOO

It is part of the traditional answer many Glaswegian damsels give to dubious nocturnal invitations and is invariably preceded by –

JIHING

Her full reply to the gentleman's proposition is –

JIHINGKAMMACOO?

I chanced to hear a young lady give such a reply to a forward fellow from outwith the city. He said "I don't get it." Quick as a flash his fair companion assured him –

BIGOADANYEDONTMAC!

The Professor

On a Glaswegian Summer Holiday

One of my most vivid memories of Glasgow is that of the lovely old city's celebrated jour de fete or, to give it its Keltic designation, the Day of Fair Setter, or Fair Setter Day.

As I hastened into the street to join in the revelry I found the air filled with the traditional festival song – "ERRARAINOANU ... SCUMMINDOONINBUCKITS!" I was advised to follow the merry throng leaving the metropolis to take train and steamship to the carnival city of Rothesay. But first, how was I to proceed thereto?

I requested directions of a sturdy young native who was resting at a street corner. Alas the youth did not appear to be versed in the English language. His only answer to my query was a lilting Gaelic phrase signifying his regret at being unable to assist me. "AWORRAL," he sighed, "AWORRAL-KNOACKYURHEIDAFF."

Fortunately a small patriarchal gentleman perceived our linguistic impasse and came to my assistance. "CENTRUL STATION," he intoned. Then, to my amazement, he commenced to conjugate one of the lesser-known Latin verbs – "GERRABUS ... NORISBUS ... ANURRABUS ... O, HEERABUS!" I complimented him on his erudition and hired a taxicab to convey me to the Central Station.

As I entered the imposing old edifice the very spirit of Mardi Gras was abroad. Still the glad cries came from the ecstatic vacationers. A large matron gave voice to what sounded to me like the rallying cry of a Highland clan – "IZFURGOATRABLIDDITICKITS!" Soon I was being carried on a wave of happy humanity towards the train.

I was not sorry to find a corner seat and I put my bowler hat down beside me. Judge of my surprise when I was addressed by two young ladies who were obviously of Burmese descent. One damsel declared, "ERRASATE." Her companion quickly riposted with "WHERRASATE?" Then the first young lady regarded me with a quizzical air and uttered a strange-sounding Eastern phrase – "ZATSATETOOK?" I could only shake my head. Suddenly, to my astonishment, the stouter of the two maidens sat down upon my hat ... However, she apologised with yet another pretty Burmese phrase – "FLYMANU SATESTOOKNOO."

At Wemyss Bay as we formed a queue for embarkation in the ship for Rothesay the word "TAKYUR!" came frequently to my ears. "TAKYURTIME!" urged a gentleman heavily burdened with luggage; "TAKYURBAGAFFMAFIT!" called a lady; and a comely maiden observed to a gallant near her ... "TAKYURHONNAFFMABUM!"

It was not long ere the ship arrived at the island paradise of Rothesay. As I walked along the promenade I was astonished by the cosmopolitan aspect of the visitors. On all sides gentlemen of the Mahommedan persuasion were calling out "ALLAH! ALLAH! ... ALLAHAWAFURRAPINT", ... "ALLA-HAWAFURRAHAUF" and "ALLAHAWANGITSTOCIOUS".

Later, in a hostelry, I was in conversation with one of these gentlemen and he told me the names of some of his fellow-travellers. I was astounded to learn that they were undoubtedly of Chinese ancestry. "See," said my new-found friend, "He is HAUF FU ... He is JISTABOOT FU and he is BUNG FU." A gentleman who had seated himself on the floor was designated FU AZZAWULK. I made bold to question Mr Fu Azzawulk as to his place of origin in Ancient China. He looked up at me and answered in the language of his forefathers – "ALHINGWAN OANYU."

I learned much during my sojourn amongst the Glaswegian natives on the glamorous island of Bute. I append a glossary of some of the more obscure words in their fascinating language.

SOFFIKOLRADAY

Today's temperature is extremely low.

SLIKRADEIDAWINTER

The temperature is reminiscent of that experienced in December.

MASPUDZIZLOUPIN

The typical summer weather has reactivated my chilblains.

RATWINZAPEST

That wind is a nuisance.

BELLAZBROLLIZBLEWOOT

Bella's umbrella has been rendered useless by the gale.

RAINZOANAGAIN

The weather is back to normal.

SJISTASHOOR

I am making an optimistic weather forecast.

SAFNU!

The downpour has ceased.

RASUNZOOT

A miracle has taken place!

The Engagement Party

Lecturer: This lecture on Glasgwegianology commences with a playlet about a young lady and her sweetheart who are attending a party to celebrate the engagement of their friend Nancy. As they stand together in a corner surveying the guests they converse in their native tongue ...

> **Girl**: It wiz nice O' Nancy invitin' us yins tae hur pairty.
>
> **Young man**: Aye.
>
> **Girl**: Therr's Nancy's financy, Wee Clancy ... a right chancer.
>
> **Young man**: Hoo can Nancy fancy rat chancer Clancy fur a financy?
>
> **Girl**: He's in ra money.
>
> **Young man**: She's in ra club.
>
> **Girl**: Haud yur bliddy tongue!
> A FEMALE IN THE BACKGROUND STARTS TO SING "VOLARE"
> Whissat noise?
>
> **Young man**: It's Carrie Balharrie singin' "Volare".
>
> **Girl**: Carrie Balharrie fancies Harry Barrie. They're gaun' ragither.
>
> **Young man**: Aw rat singin's hellish! So depressin' ... Ah waant anurra hauf.

9

Girl: So dae Ah.

Young man: (CRANING TO LOOK AT BOTTLES ON TABLE) The booze huz ran oot! Jist sody watter left! Let's go!

Girl: We canny leave yit! We're no' long here.

Young man: C'm oan doon tae ra pub. Ra baur's no' faur.

Girl: Lissen, sodyheid, Ah'm no' leavin' ... Ah'm jist thinkin'.

Young man: That's a nuvvulty.

Girl: Carrie Balharrie's dancin' wi' Harry Barrie but she's winkin' tae Gary Parry.

Young man: Look, Ah'm gaun' oot fur a hauf. You can stey an' puzzle oot the question.

Girl: Whit question?

Young man: Wull Carrie Balharrie marry Harry Barrie or Gary Parry?

Lecturer: The conversation of the young lady and her sweetheart, or lumbur, at Nancy's engagement party provides us with some interesting words and phrases. Let us examine a few of these.

It seems obvious that neither is in favour of Nancy's betrothal to the diminutive Mr Clancy. At once the young man uses the word –

HOOKIN

To this he appends a more striking word and this gives us –

HOOKINNANCIFANCIRATCHANCERCLANCIFUR-RAFINANCY?

The young lady explains the eligibility of Mr Clancy by employing what would appear to be a Persian expression –

IZZINRAMUNNI

Her escort thereupon surveys the contours of the newly-engaged maiden and announces his verdict with another Middle Eastern term –

SHEEZZINRA

Under the impression that Nancy has become a member of some organisation, he states firmly –

SHEEZZINRACLUB

His fair companion refutes the allegation that her friend is too involved in club activities and exclaims –

HODJUR

using it in conjunction with a German noun –

BLIDDITUNG

thus making the emphatic request –

HODJURBLIDDITUNG

HODJUR, of course, is used in other contexts. A lady who finds that her husband is incapacitated after partaking of refreshments may add to it a word derived from the Japanese language –

KINYINO

as she make the inquiry –

KINYINOHODJURBEVVI?

HODJUR is sometimes prefixed by the syllable "AL" and it becomes

ALHODJUR

A lady seeking to chastise another lady may avail herself of a friend's offer –

ALHODJURHONBAG

This in turn precedes another word borrowed from an obscure Indian dialect –

TIYUBASHUR

So the offer made to the aggressive lady reads –

ALHODJURHONBAGTIYUBASHUR

But let us return to the words used by the young couple at the engagement party. The young man explains to his inamorata that a female guest is rendering an Italian ballad –

CARRIBALHARRISINGINVOLARE

The damsel then discloses that Miss Balharrie has formed a romantic attachment to a Mr Barrie –

CARRIBALHARRIFANCISHARRIBARRI

She signifies that their association is a close one, using the

expressive native phrase –
RURGON RUGIRRUR
But her escort, the lumbur, is not interested in the details of Miss Balharrie's courtship. He has made the disconcerting discovery that the supply of alcoholic beverages at the party has become exhausted. He urges the young lady to accompany him to licensed premises. In a telling sentence he reveals –
RABORZNOFAUR
But his comely companion refuses to leave the function and is lost in thought, wondering why Miss Carrie Balharrie, while dancing with Mr Harry Barrie, is winking to another gentleman, a Mr Gary Parry. Her own lumbur, still anxious to visit the nearby hostelry, suggests that she should puzzle out the question for herself. "Whit question?" she inquires. In a word of the most enchanting poesy the young man enlightens her –
WULCARRIBALHARRIMARRIHARRIBARRIOR-GARRIPARRI?

The Professor

On Hogmanay

How exhilarating it was to sojourn once more in Glasgow, that charming citadel of tradition and culture. By a happy chance my arrival coincided with the ancient and picturesque Festival of Hogmanay or, as it is known in the native patois, RA BIG BOOZE-UP.

It was my good fortune to meet with a gentleman who invited me to accompany him to the sacred Hogmaniacal rites at a residence in the remote Southern terrain of the city called RASOOSIDE.

When I suggested that it might be expedient to engage a taxicab my companion mentioned a lady's name. "NORAH!" he said, "NORAHBLIDDICHANCE." Before I could question him as to the lady's identity he made certain obscure references to snow and the Yukon ... "SNOWFAUR," he stated, "YUKONHOOFIT."

Alas, the gentleman and I began to find that our safari was somewhat fatiguing. Happily we were able to take our ease in each of the seven taverns we discovered along our route. When we entered the last of these delightful havens of rest we encountered a truly festive scene. There was a merry ringing of bells and those who dispensed the refreshments were wishing their patrons well with heartfelt cries of "RABELLZWENT!" "SEFTURTIME!" and "BAURZSHUT!" A gentleman who was favouring the company with a song was courteously thanked with the old Doric word, "YUVHUDD-ANUFFMAC".

As we reached the residence that was to be the scene of the ceremonies I was full of the spirit of the old Caledonian Hogmanay Festival. What a gracious Scottish reception was accorded me by the other participants! They gathered round me and bade me welcome with the age-old Gaelic salutation – "HUZZIBRUNGA!" "HUZZIBRUNGA!" ... "HUZZIBRUNGACERRYOOT?" When I presented my hostess with a modest package of wine-gums she thanked me in the lilting language of her Hebridean forefathers. "MEANJIOL!" she murmured, "MEANJIOLBAMPOAT!"

A little later I became aware of the fact that two damsels near me were discussing the hostess. From their conversation I deduced that the lady had been engaged in a romance with a lover from some tropical clime. "She has," declared one of the damsels, "a black bun in the oven."

But it did my heart good to observe how enthusiastically those simple natives entered into the spirit of the proceedings. I noticed one stout patriarch performing a lively ceremonial dance on top of a coffee table. The onlookers signified their appreciation with ecstatic calls of "GERRIM!" ... "GERRIMAFFRATABLE!" "GERRIM OOTAHERE!" and "GERRIMTAEHISSCRATCHUR!"

The carnival was continuing with a gaiety that was contagious when, suddenly, a regrettable mishap occurred. A plump lady who had been helping to serve the refreshments became indisposed and had to be assisted to a small ante-room, or cludgie as it is called. To my horror I learned that she had inadvertently swallowed a portion of a valuable necklace. Several of my fellow-guests informed me, "She has a good bead in her."

I was relieved when, some thirty minutes later, the lady reappeared and intimated with what I took to be a Glaswegian medical term that she had made a complete recovery. "AGOATITAWUP," she disclosed. Then to my astonish-

14

ment, she made an announcement that no doubt survives from the Roman occupation of old Scotia. In fluent Latin she proclaimed, "O SEEZA SLUGATRAT BOATLARUM!"

But yet another mishap occurred. From an adjoining apartment came an agonized female shriek followed by an urgent pronouncement in the strange argot of Rasooside ... "DRAPTIZ! DRAPTIZ BOATTLE OAN MA FIT!" My surmise that something untoward had happened proved only too true when I was informed that the hostess was having her first fit in the kitchen.

My alarm was increased when a lady who had been gazing from a window turned white-faced to the gathering and in a voice that trembled with fear gave them the dread news that a symbolical harbinger of ill-fortune was about to visit them. "Black Maria is coming!" she wailed.

The very name struck terror into the Hogmanay celebrants. "Black Maria is coming!" they cried as panic-stricken, they began to flee from the house. In vain did I endeavour to calm their superstitious fears. "Fear not!" I adjured them, "I shall face up to Black Maria!" One comely maiden expressed her warm approval of my proposal. In her fascinating Highland tongue she wished me well with the haunting words – "OCHAWAN! ... OCHAWAN! ... OCHAWANGITSTUFT!"

Dining Out

Lecturer: Some picturesque examples of the native language may be heard in certain Glasgow eating houses. We begin this lesson with an excerpt from my play "STUFFINYURTURKI", or in English, "DINING OUT".

Seated at a table in a modest cafe a young man awaits the arrival of a damsel with whom he has formed a romantic attachment. A waitress approaches and regards him with disapproval.

> **Waitress**: (ASIDE) Aw, ra bliddy pest! (TO THE YOUNG MAN) Whiddje fur?
>
> **Young man**: Nuhin ra noo. Waitin' fur a burd. (HE TAKES A CIGARETTE STUB FROM BEHIND HIS EAR) Er, goarra ... goarra li'?
>
> > THE WAITRESS TAKES A BOX OF MATCHES FROM HER APRON POCKET AND HANDS IT TO HIM. THE YOUNG MAN STRIKES A MATCH. BUT, WHILE GAZING AT THE WAITRESS'S BUST, HE BECOMES DISTRAIT. HE THROWS DOWN THE MATCH SUDDENLY.
> >
> > AWGORRA nearly burnt ma snitch aff!
> >
> > THE GIRL ARRIVES AND SEATS HERSELF AT THE TABLE.

Girl: Yur therr.

Young man: Whirra hell kep' ye?

Girl: Zootra messidges fur ma murra. Bought hur a punna fresh burra.

Young man: A punna burra furra murra? Could yur wee brurra no' go furra punna burra furra? Or yur urra brurra?

Girl: Huvny goarra anurra brurra.

Young man: Aw your bahookie!

Girl: (LOOKING ROUND AT HER BOTTOM) 'Supwit?

Young man: Shut yur geggie. (TO WAITRESS) The usual.

Waitress: Pies is aff.

Girl: Can Ah've a curry?

Young man: (TO WAITRESS) Curry fur ra burd.

Waitress: S'nuttoan.

Young man: (SNATCHING MENU CARD FROM WAITRESS AND GLARING AT IT) Thur hee-haw oan! Ma goarra never seen the like. 'Saw aff! ... We're aff an' a'!

THE YOUNG MAN AND THE GIRL RISE AND LEAVE THE CAFE.

Lecturer: Let me translate and explain the delicate nuances of the words and phrases used in the cafe, or Tally's as we call it. When the young man arrives to dine he does not hear the waitress's sotto voce observation –

AURABLIDDIPEST

This word is traditionally voiced by waitresses in eating houses to indicate that the establishment is about to close for the night and the prospective diner is not wholly welcome ... Nevertheless, the waitress endeavours to ascertain the customer's requirements with the simple query ...

WHIDDJEFUR?

Note the prefix "WHIDDJE". We use this generally in the imperative sense, that is, when asking an important question.

Accordingly, a young lady may say to her escort, or lumbur,

WHIDDJEWAANT?
WHIDDJEDAEN?
WHIDDJEHINKA UM?

Of course, if the lumbur is unduly amorous the maiden may reinforce her inquiry with the more emphatic phrase ...

NUNNARAT ... CURRITOOT!

But that is by the way ... In the cafe the young man intimates to the waitress that he will postpone his repast. He employs a word that has no doubt been borrowed from our Pakistani citizens ...

NUHINRANU

When he inadvertently burns his nose with a match while surveying the waitress's physique he exclaims ...

AWGOARRA NEARLY BURNT MA SNITCH AFF!

You may have noticed that the young man has more than once used the word ...

GOARRA

When asking for the means to light his cigarette he said ...

GOARRALI?

"GOARRA" is often used when we are making a request or seeking information. So we have ...

GOARRA NEW NEEBUR?
GOARRA STORY ABOOT HUR?
GOARRA DEKATUR FANCIMAN?

When "GOARRA" is prefixed by the syllable "AW" it changes its meaning entirely. Here are some examples ...

AWGOARRA PIPE'S BURSTIT?
AWGOARRA CEILIN'S FELL IN!
AWGOARRA WIFE'S MURRA'S HERE!

But back to the cafe. The young lady enters and expresses her joy at seeing the lumbur with the rather charming greeting the Glasgow damsel reserves for her lover ...

YURTHERR

Her sweetheart is concerned that she might have lost her way and he inquires solicitously ...

18

WHIRRAHELKEPYI?

The young lady reveals that she has been purchasing a pound of butter for her mother, or as she puts it ...

APUNNABURRAFURRAMURRA

The word "FURRA" confuses most English people and other foreigners. It has several meanings – all relating to romance. A gentleman studying a photograph of a young lady in Playboy magazine might sigh ...

OFURRANIGHTWIHUR!

A young lady wishing to curtail the activities of a passionate lover would also use the word "FURRA" as she informed him ...

YURGAUNAEFURRA

In the cafe, you may remember, the lumbur cut short the lovers' tiff with the cryptic utterance ...

AWYURBAHOOKIE

This was merely an ancient word that signified the discussion was at an end. But, such are the subtleties of the language, even the young Glasgow lady misunderstood him. She believed he was being critical of the rear portion of her anatomy. So she demands to know ...

SUPWIT?

Her escort, however, simply advises her to preserve a dignified silence. He uses one of our age-old phrases ...

SHUTYUR GEGGIE

He could have conveyed his request by employing a variety of delightful words, such as ...

ACHSHURRIT
CLEYUP
GIEYURJAWAREST

and

PIRRASOACKINIT

However, the young man goes on to ask the waitress to serve their usual dinner. She responds with a word obviously borrowed from the Russian language ...

PYZIZAFF

Prompted by his inamorata, he orders another dish ...

CURRIFURRABURD

When the young gentleman discovers that there is little or nothing listed on the menu card he ends the visit to the cafe with the trenchant declaration ...

SAWAFFANWEERAFFANAW!

The Professor

On Mating Habits

On a recent visit to the great metropolis on the Clyde I was fortunate enough to witness the strange ritual courtship engaged in by certain of the young natives.

In a busy thoroughfare I took note of two young maidens, or "burds", guardedly scrutinising a pair of young males who had come into view. The young braves flaunted their gaily-coloured raiment and hair arranged in spikes and made their presence known to the females with the plaintive cry ...

HEH-HINGMI!

The word "HING-MI" plays no small part in the conversation of the natives whose desire it is to mate. Indeed, from one of the colourful males I heard it used in the plural ...

HINGMIZ

Gazing fondly upon one of the damsels who was extremely well-proportioned he uttered the haunting love-call ...

SHIHUZSUMPERRAHINGMIZ

I took it that he was referring to the lustrous eyes of the young lady. She at once replied to his call with the Gaelic word ...

OCHONE

embellishing it with the pretty expression ...

YURWEY YANYUK

And so the full beauty of her answering call came to me ...

OCHONE YURWEY YANYUK!

With eyes shyly averted the maidens continued on their

way. Then the other male adolescent delivered himself of the manly mating-cry ...

GONNIGEESE

He was obviously likening the two "burds" to those of the feathered variety. He continued his ornithological theme with ...

GONNIGEESE ADATEHEN?

The objects of their affection appeared to heed not the urgent cries. It seemed to me as if the courtship were doomed to failure. Then suddenly one of the prepossessing maidens turned round to face the wooers. From her lips came the romantic love-call that doubtless has echoed down the Highland glens from time immemorial. It began with the exotic-sounding ...

AWAYNGIT

and was completed with the monosyllabic ...

WAASHT

so that the love-call in its entirety was ...

AWAYNGITWAASHT

Ah, what ecstasy there was in the voices of the two young males as they responded to the young lady's heartfelt request. Triumphantly they demonstrated their joy with exultant chorus ...

YAPERRA! YAPERRA!
YAPERRAHERRIES!

As the two maidens were vanishing into the Keltic twilight they continued to call encouragement to their eager suitors. Their sweet girlish voices were raised in an old Caledonian love-song which began with the word ...

YIZZIZZA

I listened entranced as the poetic invitation filled the night air with its lyrical loveliness ...

YIZZIZZACUPLADAMGOATS,
YIZZIZZACUPLABAMPOATS.

Delighted, the two young cavaliers replied with great fervour ...

AWGUIDRIDDINZ,
YAPERRAMIDDINZ!

Consumer Affairs

Lecturer: The rich Glaswegian language is heard at its most beautiful when native speakers are discussing consumer affairs. We illustrate this lesson with an introductory playlet in which we see a young lady and her fiancé making various purchases in a supermarket.

> **Young lady:** Wherra hell did you get tae?
> **Fiancé:** Did ye no' see me at the wine coonter?
> **Young lady:** 'Sat yuv goat therr?
> **Fiancé:** 'Sa boa' 'la scud. Gi'es ye a rerr glow.
>   (HE PUTS BOTTLE IN HER BASKET AND TAKES FROM IT A JAR OF JELLY) ... Whissis ye've goat, Mattie?
> **Young lady:** 'Sa jaura jeelly.
>   FIANCÉ PUTS THE JAR OF JELLY BACK IN BASKET.
>   YOUNG LADY TAKES PURSE FROM BASKET, PUTS BASKET ON FLOOR AND RUMMAGES THROUGH PURSE.
> **Young lady:** Ah'm a bit shoart.
> **Fiancé:** Ah know ... Ye're wee but gemme
> **Young lady:** Ah need a p.
> **Fiancé:** It's aw rat shandy ye hud.
> **Young lady:** Ya bampoat! 'Sa PENNY Ah need!

Fiancé: (TAKING JAR OF PATÉ from basket) Heh, whissis?

Young lady: 'Sa jaura pait.

Fiancé: Ye don't cry it "pait" ... It's "pâté" Mattie.

Young lady: Then why huv thae pit "pate" oan the jaur fur?

Fiancé: 'Cos the French don't say "pait" They say "pâté", Mattie.

Young lady: Well Ah'm no' French ... Ah've ate pait an' a wee tait o' pait oan a plate's great wi' a pataity.

Fiancé: Ye're batty, Mattie. Rat pâté wi' a tattie'll mak ye a fatty, Mattie.

Lecturer: Let us study the conversational exchanges between the young lady and her fiancé, or "hur intendit" as he is called, in the supermarket.

When the young lady, Mattie, discovers that her fiancé has strayed from her side she uses the well-known Glaswegian word ...

JIJU

To it she puts the prefix ...

WHERRAHEL

Then she adds ...

GERRY

And so she inquires of the young gentleman ...

WHERRAHELJIJUGERRY?

a lady seeking her husband's aid on finding that the glass containing her dentures has vanished from her bedside table will preface her query with the word ...

JIJU

adding a few more syllables to it to give us ...

JIJUSEEMAWALLISKICKINABOOT?

to which her husband may well reply ...

JIJUNOPITREMOANRAMANTELPIECE?

When the young lady in the supermarket observes that her fiancé is in possession of a bottle she addresses him with the Russian-sounding word ...

SATYUV

to which she appends ...

GOATRERR

thus completing the question ...

SATYUVGOATRERR?

The young gentleman discloses that he has visited the wine department from which he has selected a bottle of wine or, as he puts it, ...

BOALASCUD

He gives his opinion of its quality with the technical expression ...

GEEZYARERRGLO

As he places the bottle in the wire basket he displays an interest in the contents of the latter. He takes from the basket one of the purchases and questions the damsel about it. In her explanation she borrows from the Spanish language and says ...

SAJORRA

SAJORRAJEELI

At this juncture the young lady discovers that she does not quite have the sum required as payment for her groceries. She informs her escort ...

AMSHOART

He, believing that she is referring to her diminutive stature, pays her a graceful compliment ...

YURWEEBUTGEMME

But the maiden has no time for compliments. She points out that she needs one penny or, in the colloquial parlance, "a p." Once again her "intendit" misunderstands her. He contends that certain refreshments she has consumed have discommoded her. Employing what would appear to be an Indian word, he alleges ...

SAWRATSHANDIYEHUD

The young lady hotly refutes the suggestion. Meanwhile the fiancée extracts another of her purchases from the basket and desires her to identify it. Again she uses the Spanish word ...

SAJORRA
SAJORRAPAIT

Her companion ruminates over her use of the word "pait". Then he realises her mistake and corrects her with two trenchant words ...

SNOPAIT, SPATTIMATTI

His fiancée resents his criticism and declines to adopt the French pronunciation. She goes on to extol the appetising nature of the product. In syllables of the purest poesy she assures him ...

AVATEPAITANAWEETAITAPAITOANAPLATESG-
REATWIAPATAITY

The young man is fearful of the dire effect this culinary melange will have on his loved one's girth. He questions her sanity in eating pâté with potato and cries out the warning ...

YURBATTIMATTI RATPATTIWIATATTIALMAKYE-
AFATTIMATTI!

The Professor

At a Hallowe'en Party

My semantical and anthropological research obliged me to pay yet another visit to the great city of Glasgow. To me its fascination derives from the aura of Keltic mysticism that pervades it.

Accordingly I was all agog when, on visiting one of the city's quaint old hostelries, or "boozers" as they are termed, I met a gentleman who appeared to be completely au fait with the customs and language of his native habitat.

He spoke of a strange mystic rite which was to be performed that very evening in the remote clan stronghold of Castle Milk.

"To whom," I enquired, "is this ceremony dedicated?"

"Sally Een," my companion revealed.

I had not heard of Sally Een but I concluded that she was one of those enchanting figures with which the folklore of Old Scotia is so richly endowed. Not so well-known, perhaps, as those other legendary heroines, Mesdames Fran and Anna, La Lulu and the tragic lady known as Auntie Mary who had such trouble with her recalcitrant canary.

I intimated to my new-found friend that I was more than anxious to pay tribute to Sally Een. Lapsing into his native Glasgois, he uttered an explanation of surprise ...

"SAPERTI!"

Then impulsively he issued the invitation ...

"SUP AT RA FANCY WUMMAN'S!"

I assured him that I would be honoured to sup at the abode of The Fancy Wumman. I particularly desired to meet the high priestess who was to officiate at the Ceremony of Sally Een. Without further ado we proceeded to the gathering-place.

The door of the house was opened by a lady whom I at once recognised as The Fancy Wumman. Her multicoloured hair was garnished with picturesque metal cylinders and her face was painted in vivid shades of peach and red and an electrifying blue was daubed on the lids of her eyes.

She greeted my escort by name, crying ...

IT'S SAUL!

IT'S SAUL SODYHEID!

Quickly Mr Sodyheid whispered to her what I took to be a Gaelic password ...

ERRAKERRYOOT

Thereupon The Fancy Wumman relieved me of the large paper container filled with bottles and cans which custom had obliged me to purchase in the hostelry. Then we joined the participants in the tribal rite. Already the solemn proceedings had commenced.

A comely damsel was kneeling upon a chair. She was in the act of causing a fork to fall from her lips into a sacrificial font filled with water in which floated a quantity of apples. There was a tense silence as the symbolic fork descended quickly to the bottom of the font.

The young lady gazed down in pious meditation at the apples, then, throwing back her head, she gave vent to an incantation ...

RADAMPT! RADAMPTFOARKSBLUNTASBUGRI!

Next an aged gentleman declared that he too wished to play his part in the awe-inspiring ritual. I was greatly moved by the devoutness in his tones as he proclaimed ...

HERESHOOTI! HERESHOOTI DOOKFURAIPPLES!

With tender care the other devotees of Sally Een assisted the patriarch to kneel upon the chair. Reverently, the handle of the fork was placed between his lips. A moment later came a clattering sound from the font. The old gentleman looked up, toothless, and from all sides came the inspiring chorus of acclamation ...

IZWALLIZFELOOTWIRRAFOARK!

I observed other touching acts of devotion at the gathering.

One of these, it transpired, called for a statuesque maiden wearing an abbreviated skirt to seat herself upon a large specially-prepared scone which had been placed on an armchair. She then rose quickly and uttered a traditional call first heard centuries ago during the Franco-Scottish alliance ...

MERCI!

She at once added another word to give the elaborate incantation ...

MERCIZAWTRAICLE!

The ceremonial continued in all its Caledonian majesty and reached a triumphant climax when the lady known as The Fancy Wumman plunged headfirst into the water amongst the apples. This was the signal for the other participants in the celebration to hail her as their goddess. They chorused fervently...

GODDESS! GODDESS!
GODDESS MUNSE SINCE SHE HUDDA WAASH!

The solemn observances came to an end when the devotees of Sally Een assumed their grotesque tribal masks or, as their patois has it, "fause faces".

I made bold to congratulate the young lady in the short skirt on her mask. "Never," I assured her, "have I seen such a repulsive countenance." Graciously, in the lilting language of her island forefathers, she acknowledged my felicitations concerning her "fause face". She trilled ...

GOARUMNO
GOARUMNO WERRINWAN!

When eventually I took my departure she bade my farewell with the charming Gaelic words ...

YAULSCUNNUR YURAFFYURRUDDICHUMP!

The Contretemps

Lecturer: Some of the most intriguing words in the lovely lilting language of Glasgow are heard when natives of the city become involved in some sort of contretemps. This fact may be demonstrated in the playlet we use for this lesson.

The locale is a street and there a buxom maiden is in attendance at a barrow from which she is selling a variety of fruit and vegetables.

A young man known as THE FLY FELLA enters.

Fly fella: (LOOKING BEHIND HIM) Whirra hell's ra marra?
     HIS SWEETHEART, OR BURD, ENTERS. SHE IS FATIGUED AND HER FEET APPEAR TO BE CAUSING HER SOME DISCOMFORT.

Burd: An canny go nae farra.

Fly fella: Here Clarra wi' hur barra! Take a sate oan ra haun'le o' ra barra.

Burd: 'Stoo narra.

Fly fella: So 'tis. (GLANCING AT BURD'S REAR) That's some jaxi ye've oan ye.

Burd: 'Sno' as big as your heid.
     BOTH SURVEY THE FRUIT ON THE BARROW. THE FLY FELLA FINGERS TWO MELONS.

Barrow-girl: Haun's aff ra melons!

Fly fella: Ah never laid a finger oan ye! (HE NOTICES A MARROW) Heh, zarra marra oan yur barra, Clarra?

Barrow-girl: (SARCASTICALLY) 'Sno' a tamarra.

Fly fella: (POÍNTING TO GROUND) A tamarra's tummul't ootra barra, Clarra.

Burd: Ah think Ah'll buy ra marra fur ma farra. Mia Farra bought a marra fur hur farra.

Fly fella: S'ootra question. Whit's YOUR farra waant wi' a marra affa barra?

    BURD PICKS UP THE MARROW

Barrow-girl: (SHOUTS) Pirrat marra back!

    BURD, STARTLED, DROPS THE MARROW ON THE BARROW. THE BARROW GOES OVER WITH A CRASH.

Fly fella: Aw, Mia Farra's cowped Clarra's barra wi' a marra!

Lecturer: Some of the words and phrases used in the playlet may sound strange to non-Glaswegians. The Fly Fella betrays some anxiety about the young lady with whom he has been strolling. He wishes to know what is troubling her and inquires solicitously ...

WHIRRA HELZA MARRA?

Note the key-word ...

HELZA

This is frequently heard at social functions. Thus ...

WHENRA HELZA PERTY STERTIN'?
WHYRA HELZA BURDS NO' HERE?
WHERRA HELZA BOOZE?

But back to our playlet. You may recall that the Fly Fella made an interesting allusion to the rearward contours of the young lady's anatomy, observing "That's some jaxi ye've oan ye!"

YU-VOAN-YE

This introduces to us the descriptive words ...

VOAN, ZOAN and TOAN

These invariably relate to the physiological aspects of a person. A young man-about-town commenting on the physical attributes of a young lady will say ...

SOMEBOADISHE ZOAN UR!

But his friend, more fastidious than he, might exclaim ...

LUKATRAFA TOAN UR!

And, of course, there is the phrase often used when a Glaswegian native is confronted by an unusually rotund lady or gentleman ...

WHIRRAKYTEYU VOAN YE!

Now we come to the rather dramatic part of our playlet – when the Fly Fella discovers the vegetable marrow reposing in the barrow. At once he utters the lovely phrase ...

ZARRA MARRA OANRA BARRA CLARRA?

Remember "ZARRA" is employed when we wish to find out something, as in ...

ZARRA FACMAC?

Meaning – "Is that the case, stranger?" Sometimes we may be confused as to a person's identity. Again we use "ZARRA". A long-haired individual in a dimly-lit discotheque might occasion the query ...

ZARRA CHICKORRA HERRIWULLI?

Again, an amorous damsel could use the word romatically to her bashful lover ...

ZARRA BESYEKINDAE?

Next I want to draw your attention to another charming word. It was used when the Fly Fella noticed that a tomato had fallen from the fruit barrow ...

A TAMARRA'S TUMMUL-TOOTRA BARRA!

The important word here is ...

TUMMUL-TOOTRA

We also have ...

TUMMUL-TINTERA

A lady who had been accidentally precipitated into a rubbish depository may be said to have...

TUMMUL-TINTERA MIDDIN

But we have many words bearing the prefix ...

TUMMUL

such as ...

TUMMUL-TAFFRA

A gentleman who met with a mishap after dining and wining would be reported as having ...

TUMMUL-TAFFRA CHERR

A word new in our vocabulary stems from the permissive society. Referring to a lady and gentleman meeting for the first time we make use of ...

TUMMUL-TINTY

To this we add the Latin word ...

RAPERRAREM

And so we have the interesting statement ...

RAPERRAREM TUMMUL-TINTY BED

When the young lady in the playlet wishes to purchase the marrow for her father her escort tells her brusquely ...

SOOTRA QUESTION

The word ...

SOOTRA

would be heard from the young lady if she came to realise that the ungallant Fly Man was not a suitable associate for her. She would preface it with the word ...

YURBUM

She would then deliver herself of the trenchant declaration that has come from the lips of many a Glaswegian maiden disillusioned with her male acquaintance ...

YURBUMSOOTRAWINDAE!

The Professor

Attends a Wedding Reception

I had deemed it no small honour that the members of a learned society should ask me to address them on the fruits of my Glasgovian researches. Alas, Fate ordained that I should not appear before the distinguished gathering. By a complete mischance I found myself in a different edifice from that which I had intended to visit.

To a gentleman standing at the portals I confessed that I had lost my bearings. To my surprise he clapped me upon the shoulder and with the utmost good humour declared ...

AH, MISTA WEY!

I, of course, informed him that I was not Mr Wey. The gentleman, however, did not appear to hear me. In the strange but appealing argot of the Eastern province of Brigton he bade me a cordial welcome, crying ...

JEEZYURSTOCIOUS!

and forthwith he marched me triumphantly into the hall. Great was my astonishment and delight when I perceived that I was attending a highly-important Scottish ceremony ...

THE FEAST OF RAWADDIN

Yes, it was a typical Scottish wedding fiesta. With the other celebrants I awaited the arrival of the newly-espoused couple. A gasp of surprise arose when the bride entered unaccompanied or, in the native idiom ...

OANURBLIDDITOD

Some concern was shown by the matriarch of the bride's clan, a venerable lady who was referred to by her title ...

HURAULGRANNI

In a voice that rang through the hall the matriarch called ...

WHERRAHELZAGROOM

In accordance with custom she was answered by a diminutive gentleman known variously by the company as ...

RABBESMAN or
BOWLIWEEBACHLE

He revealed the whereabouts of the bridegroom. In a charming old Gaelic rhyme he announced ...

RABUGGRULNOBUDGE
OOTRABLOOMINCLUDGE

It transpired that the bridegroom had been overcome by emotion and had retired to an ante-room. But in less than an hour he appeared, pale and a little unsteady in his gait. Once again came a call from ...

HURAULGRANNI

She welcomed the young man to the company, calling him by what appeared to be her pet name for him ...

GLAIKITNYAFF

What pride was in her tones as she hailed him with ...

GLAIKITNYAFF YURBEVVID!

Next came the ceremonial partitioning of the wedding cake. With grave demeanour the newly-wedded damsel took up a large knife and inserted it in the impressive confection. Then softly from her lips came a mystic Incantation, a plea for connubial bliss that doubtless her ancestors had voiced many centuries before ...

HORDUZ!
HORDUZ ABLIDDIBRICK!

To assist her in the solemn rite the bridegroom, whose name I gathered was "Pete", placed his hand over that of his bride. I was deeply moved when she looked shyly at her nuptial partner and made to him what was obviously an age-old pledge of devotion ...

FURRALUVVAPETE
YURHAUNZASWEET

It was not long ere I became aware of another participant in the ceremonies. I understood her name to be ...

HURMURRA

She listened intently as a gentleman raised his glass in a toast to the bride and bridegroom. In his native language he intoned ...

GUIDLUCKYIZZILNEEDIT!

At this juncture the lady known as ...

HURMURRA

bent her head in silent prayer. She then commenced a tribal chant in praise of the sweetness of the married state. What sincerity there was in her voice as she sang ...

O MOLASSES! O MOLASSES!

I was quick to note the aptness of the word as she continued with the lovely old ballad ...

O MOLASSESMERRITAHEIDCASE!

Overwhelmed by the sentimental nature of the occasion the bride became faint and was helped to a chair. So affected was she that she did not know the name of the establishment in which the wedding celebration was being held. Tremulously she asked ...

WHERRUMMA?

Without hesitation the information was given to her by ...

HURMURRA

She began with the obscure word ...

YURINRA

Then she added a word that made everything clear to the bride. Gaily she cried ...

YURINRA PUDNCLUB!

Thespians in Trouble

English producers, actresses and actors may encounter certain difficulties when endeavouring to present Scottish plays in the theatre or on television.

This is illustrated in the following sketch in which some people from south of the Border are seen rehearsing Part I of a Scottish drama series for television.

Scene: A television studio somewhere in Scotland;
Cast: BASIL, an English producer;
AUBREY, an English actor;
BRENDA, an English actress;
GLASGOW GIRL

Basil: Well, let's get going ... You'll notice the action takes place in the Scotch highlands, round about Falkirk, or some such village. Now we've got to bring out the undertones of Keltic tragedy and the mystique of the Gaelic character.

Aubrey: Basil, I'm not awfully sure about some of the words ...

Basil: Not sure? Damn it all, Aubrey, you should know the Scotch lingo by this time! You've been a whole week in Glasgow ... Let's do the scene with Brenda and you in the West End.

Brenda: (PEERING AT HER SCRIPT) It says here

"SINGLE-end".

Basil: Yes ... Well, that'll be their name for the West End. We're in a bothy – that's some sort of castle – and there's an open fire with porridge, bannocks and whatnot boiling away in a pot. In a corner of the lounge sits an old Gaelic crone.

Brenda: That's me.

Basil: Yes, you're Morag. She has a clan title, Morag the Toerag ... Now, where are we? Ah yes. Sumass, her son, goes to the window ... Go on, Aubrey.

Aubrey: (GOES TO WINDOW AND READS FROM SCRIPT) "The tatties are biling all over the range" ... Basil, what exactly are tatties?

Basil: Eh? ... Oh ... er ... they're birds of ill-omen, like albatrosses, you know. So I think you should be terror-stricken as you look out on the moor and see the tatties wheeling about.

Aubrey: I see ... "The tatties are biling all over the range" ... Do they have ranges in Scotland?

Basil: Never mind that ... Brenda, you show you're frightened too.

Brenda: Oh yes ... "Ockone! Ockone! I am terrible!" Oh, sorry ... "I am terrible fee-art!"

Basil: Go on, Aubrey. You try to comfort her.

Aubrey: (TO BRENDA) "Do not bother your ginger, hen."

Basil: (CALLS TO SIDE OF STAGE) I say, have you got the ginger hen?

GLASGOW GIRL ENTERS AND SHOWS HIM A BROWN HEN.

Good, good. (TO AUBREY AND BRENDA) The ginger hen is another symbolic bird. But we don't need it yet. (TO GIRL) Put it in my office.

GIRL EXITS WITH HEN

(TO AUBREY) You go back to the window,

Aubrey. You feel that some frightful catastrophe is going to happen. Go on.

Aubrey: (READING) "Er ... the lickt is fading fast and I canna see my brither's boattie on the lock."

Basil: Come ON, Brenda!

Brenda: Just a sec ... Ah, here we are. (READS) "Wae is me! Me laddeh is drooned in the lock! Me laddeh who was to have wad Flora Col-cue-hown. She wad have been sick ..."

Basil: Surely not SICK!

Brenda: Sorry! ... "She wad have been sic a prood bride, a gay prood bride."

Basil: Just a moment. Gay prude bride? I don't quite understand how she could be gay AND a prude ... Oh well, go on.

Brenda: "There will be nae wadding now ... er ... noo, nae C. Liddell. Me laddeh aye liked to gang to C.Liddell's ... "

Aubrey: Basil, who is this character, C. Liddell?

Basil: (IMPATIENTLY) It's not a character. It's a sea-lid – C.E.I.L.I.D.H. Some sort of game the Scotch peasants play... Please, let's get on with it! Aubrey, I want you to ...

    GLASGOW GIRL ENTERS

Girl: Hey Jimmy.

Basil: How dare you interrupt me in the middle of a rehearsal!

Girl: Keep ra heid, Mac.

Aubrey: What on earth is she saying?

Basil: I've no idea WHAT she's saying. (TO GIRL) What do you want?

Girl: Nuchin' ... Thur a fulla oana phone fur ye.

Basil: What IS she saying?

Brenda: It's Greek to me!

Girl: Ya shoo'ra chancers, diz nane o' yiz unnerstaun' plain English?

The Professor

Pays a Tribute to Rabbie

In a Glasgovian tavern I was refreshing myself with that delightful Scottish drink, a "hoffannahoff", when a venerable native scholar hailed me with a salutation which survives from the time of the Roman occupation of his country. He cried ...

O CAESAR!

To this he added a word to give me the splendid greeting in full ...

O CAESARAFIVER

He gave me to understand that on payment of £5 I could be a guest at a supper party in honour of a Scottish literary gentleman by the name of "Rabbie".

I was discomfited at having to confess that I had not heard of Mr Rabbie. Great was my astonishment when my aged acquaintance intimated to me that Mr Rabbie had been corresponding with a Canadian quadruped. Yes, he disclosed, "Rabbie wrote to a moose." I ventured to inquire if he had received a reply to his epistle; but the gentleman was reticent on the subject. He looked at me solemnly and intoned ...

TWIDGIEYIRABOAK

Without further ado the aged scholar and I repaired to the literary salon where we were to pay tribute to the illustrious Mr Rabbie.

Seated at a long table in the salon was a concourse of

erudite gentlemen. Already they were proposing toasts to various Scottish men of letters, such as Mr Poosie Nancy, Messrs Birks of Aberfeldy and an author of Irish descent, Mr Tam O'Shanter.

Not a few of the guests present were apparently of Russian origin. On all sides were mentioned the names ...

AMFURRAHOFF, GIEZAHOFF and SEEZAHOFF

A guest who kept leaving the company precipitately then returning bore the impressive Slavonic cognomen ...

MOSCOW TAERALAVVI

The carnival of Caledonian culture continued with a gaiety that was contagious. Loud and long came the celebratory cries that have made the rafters ring at many an assemblage of the Scottish intelligentsia ...

WHERRZAWINE? MAGLESSIZEMPY!
AMBEVVID! PETESPUKIN!

I made so bold as to inquire of the chairman as to when we might expect the arrival of Mr Rabbie. A sudden deep silence ensued and all eyes were upon me. Then, to my unutterable gratification, the chairman solemnly conferred on me an ancient Highland title. "You," he declared, "are the real Chieftain of the Pudden Race." So saying, he urged that the distinguished guests should all heed me, crying in ringing tones ...

AULHEIDCASE!

A few minutes later I again had cause to marvel at the cosmopolitan nature of the gathering. A request for silence came from a diminutive gentleman, or wee bachle as he was known to the cognoscenti present. He announced his intention of regaling us with what I understood to be an Indian song ...

RASH TARA

To my regret the singer was so overcome by the poignancy of the Eastern ballad that he was able only to give voice to one haunting line ...

RASH TARA RABBIBURNS

41

Nevertheless my supper companions showed their appreciation of his gallant effort with the appropriate Indian felicitation ...

IZDENCHURZ HUZFELOOT

Soon came the strains of the bagpipes. But the bagpiper too found the grandeur of the occasion too much for him. He had some difficulty in amassing sufficient wind for his instrument. But the chairman rose and proudly identified the bagpiper for us, proclaiming ...

HE IS STOCIOUS

Carried away by the sheer pageantry of the spectacle I too greeted the bagpiper with a hearty ...

HAIL, MR STOCIOUS!

Unfortunately, in my enthusiasm, I jolted the arm of a stout gentleman in cook's attire. Thereupon a large grey sphere he was carrying before him on a salver flew through the air and disintegrated on the chairman's countenance. From the onlookers came excited exclamations of ...

IZDRAPTRABLIDDIHAGGIS!

With that came the ritual that terminated the literary evening. A gentleman with the word "Hallkeeper" emblazoned on his headgear made his entrance. In a stentorian voice he called ...

OOTRALOTOYIZ! OOTORALGETRAPOLIS!

And as we poured from the premises into the friendly darkness of the Glasgwegian night we could hear him giving us the old Gaelic blessing ...

YASHOORASOAKS! GOADPEETIYIZ!

From

The Concise Parliamo Dictionary
of Current Glaswegian

The following list of the more obscure Glaswegian words and phrases with approximate definitions in ordinary English may be of some use to non-Scots who visit the great cultural metropolis on the Clyde.

> SHURSEL, HULLAWRERR, YURTHERR: Words of greeting.
> GOARA, used in various contexts, as follows –
> GOARAMDRI, an acute thirst has assailed me.
> GOARAFAGOANYE, a request for a cigarette.
> GOARAHELL, used when declining to give the importunate person a cigarette.

Various terms are used by the natives when discussing the vagaries of the weather.

> SWAARMRADAY, the temperature has risen.
> RASUNZOOT! a miracle has taken place!
> SPELTINARAIN, we have returned to normal climatic conditions.
> SELLUVAKOLNOO, the temperature has now fallen.
> MASPUDZIZFROZE, my feet are extremely cold.

Many Glaswegians seek their holiday pleasures abroad. Foreign doctors might find it advisable to acquaint themselves with some of the terms used in describing the symptoms of various ailments.

MADIALZBEALIN, some skin is no longer adhering to my face.

MACHAMPURZIZBROON, even my dentures are sunburnt.

AVAHEIDANAHOF, the modestly-priced wine is stronger than I thought.

AVASERRKYTE, I am suffering from stomach pains.

AMOFFI PEELIWALLI, the large seafood meal I ate has made mefeel somewhat frail.

ASATOANA DAUDAGLESS, I failed to notice the broken wine bottle before I sat down on the beach.

On their return from a sojourn in mainland Spain or Majorca many Glasgow natives display their snapshots with pride. Expressions that accompany their photographic exhibition are –

WANNISEE WURPHOTIES? can I induce you to suffer an hour of extreme boredom?

ERRMAMURRAPAIDLIN, that is a study of my mother seeking a sea-water easement of her painful corns.

WEEFELLA BELLAFELLINWI, a small gentleman who took Bella out in a pedalo which capsized.

RAWEANFLINGIN SAUNABOOT, the child merrily throwing sand about.

SKELPINFURRAWEAN, father cutting short the child's enjoyment.

MAWYELLINHURHEIDAFF, my mother has inadvertently sat on a bee, wasp or hornet.

Foreign students of our language are surprised to find that it contains words which are apparently of Japanese origin. A common greeting is –

HEHYU or HIYU

Other words borrowed from the Land of the Rising Sun are –

44

OBI JINGSAM WABBIT, I am exceedingly fatigued.

WANNA SUKAT, as in the hospitable invitation "Do you want a suck at my orange?"

GONNIGEISHASANG? are you going to favour us with a ballad?

UCHAMSHI, I am somewhat diffident.

WHITWUNNA HREETHURTI? a request for racing information.

OMI WHITATUMMI, a comment made on observing a gentleman's pendulous stomach.

SAMURAI BUNGFU, a lady's rebuke to her bibulous husband, Sam.

Language of Romance

Lecturer: Romance, of course, plays an important part in the lives of the young Glaswegian natives and it has its own distinctive and delightful phraseology. This is illustrated in a short scene from my latest play "The Flowering of Love", or to give it its Scottish title, "Bagzapashin".

We see two of the characters, Jimmy and his wife Nell, at a social function in the course of which they survey a young lady and gentleman who are enthusiastically demonstrating their high regard for one another.

> Jimmy: Look at ra baith o' rem! Snoggin' in front o' the hale cump'ny!
> Nell: S'awri', ra baith o rem's winchin'.
> Jimmy: Ra baith o' rem's aff thur chumps ... Oh fur Goad's sake, they're still at it. It wid gie ye ra boak!
> Nell: Stoap lukkin' at them then.
> Jimmy: Ach let's beat it an' go fur a hauf.

Lecturer: Now it is patently obvious that Jimmy, a sensitive gentleman, does not approve of the uninhibited conduct of the damsel and her lover or, as he terms them,
RABAITHOREM
The wife Nell takes a laissez-faire attitude and points out

that the young couple have formed a romantic liaison, or, as she puts it ...

RABAITHOREMZWINCHIN

Jimmy is not at all impressed by this disclosure and employs the word –

ZAFFRUR

incorporating it in the sinister sentence ...

RABAITHOREMZAFFRURCHUMPS

Thus he indicates that, in his opinion, the demonstrative lovers are lacking in mental stability.

ZAFFRUR

is also used when speaking of an incorrigible person, or heidcase. Of him it may be said that he is ...

ZAFFRURRAILS

On the other hand a lady will speak of her teetotal husband with approbation as she reveals that he is ...

ZAFFRURUM

But back to our play. As the young persons plight their troth with continuous osculation they cause Jimmy to give vent to a religious proclamation ...

OFURGOADSAKE!

Note the prefix ...

OFUR

The addition of a single letter can change its meaning entirely. Like Jimmy, a gentleman urging his wife to accompany him to a hostelry for some refreshment will use the word ...

GOFUR

as he suggests that they ...

GOFUR AHOFURTU

As often as not his spouse will be quick to reply that she is ...

NOFUR AHOFURTU.

Should her husband attempt to borrow money from her for the purchase of refreshments she is likely to make use of the following derivatives ...

DOFUR, GOFUR, HOFUR, SOFUR and LOFUR

To these she adds certain other words to make her meaning absolutely clear. So she intimates to him that she has no cash for alcoholic beverages and requests him to forget his financial proposition ...

AVNO DOFUR TAE GOFUR A HOFURTU, SOFUR GERRITYA LOFUR.

The wife will also be annoyed if her young son uses the forbidden word ...

POFUR

as in his innocent question ...

WHITSA POFUR?

But I digress. You may remember that our character Jimmy gave utterance to the lovely old word ...

GIEYIRA

It occurred in his statement that the over-amorous machinations of the young lovers would induce a feeling of nausea in all who witnessed them. He declared that they would ...

GIEYIRA BOAK.

GIEYIRA

is not infrequently heard in certain social circles and even on the football field. When one individual seeks to incapacitate another he will issue the warning ...

AL GIEYIRA HEID

Later in the play the loving young couple adjourn to a discotheque. There the youthful Lothario discovers that the sum of £2 in the new coinage has vanished through a hole in his trouser pocket. His cry of dismay rings out ...

GOARAVWENT IN LOASTTWOPOUNBITS!

A short-sighted lady who finds herself by mistake in a masculine stronghold will also give voice to ...

GOARAVWENTIN

Her discomfiture at her social gaffe will be expressed in the agonised cry ...

GOARAVWENTIN TAERAGENTS!

An equally disconcerting mishap attends the maiden in our play. While dancing energetically in the discotheque she stops suddenly and renders the haunting lament ...

GOARAVWENTIN
SPLITRASEAMS
OMAJEANS

Soon she delivers herself of an even more tragic verse. It begins with the heart-rending cry ...

RERSIZ

followed by ...

OOTMABLIDDISLAX

And so the full extent of the calamity is conveyed in the touching refrain ...

RERSIZ OOTMABLIDDISLAX!

The Professor

On a Shopping Expedition

I was more than delighted when, quite by chance, I found myself in the establishment of a small trader and made some valuable discoveries concerning the enchanting patois spoken by the natives of the great city on the Clyde.

I had been invited to a small gathering in the home of a resident in the impressive boulevard known as RAGALLA-GATE. Custom decreed that I should take with me what is termed ALITRORAMAMMIMINE. So there I was in the modest premises, or BEERSHOPE, in search of a bottle of wine.

The establishment was crowded with ladies and gentlemen purchasing various beverages for their delectation at the week-end. No sooner had I entered when I found myself in close proximity to a stout matron. Judge of my perturbation when she turned to me and made the grave allegation that I was guilty of moral turpitude. Looking at me intently, she cried ... "HOOR!"

Then suddenly to my great relief she revealed that she was indulging in a guessing game. She put the question ... "HOORYESHUVVIN?" I had to confess that I was quite ignorant of her identity. She herself enlightened me and told that her name was LENA FAMMUHURDIZ. I responded at once with a hearty "How do you do, Madam Fammuhurdiz?" Alas, the lady had quickly lost interest in the guessing game.

She turned to the damsel behind the counter and complained about the delay in being served. To my astonishment the ensuing conversation was conducted in what I had no doubt was the language of ancient Rome. The large lady observed ... "AMGERRINRATTI". From the serving maiden came the reply ... "AVONLI WANPERRAHONS".

The conversation was terminated by Madam Fammu-hurdiz taking her leave of the shoplass with the expressive Gaelic phrase "STUFFYOONYURROATTONSHOPE!" As she hastened from the beershope the large lady bade me farewell with the not dissimilar word, "STUFFYOONAWYA-MUG!"

Soon the damsel behind the counter was devoting her attentionto a housewife and her small daughter who, it appeared bore the name "Hannah". The housewife ad-dressed the serving maiden as "Anna". The linguistic prowess of the Glaswegian native was strikingly de-monstrated when the young mother spoke in Japanese. Vivaciously she hailed the shoplass with "HAWANNA!" Next she made her wants known with "AWANNABANA-NAFURMAHANNAH". From across the counter came the reply in the authentic argot of Tokyo – "YIJISWAANTRA WANBANANAHANNA?" The banana was handed over and the housewife indicated that she wished to purchase a pan loaf ... "ANAWANNAPANANNA ".

Then she remembered a request made to her by her husband, Dan, a lover of football. Dan had directed her to bring him a can of liquid sustenance. She pointed to the can and again came the accents of the Far East ... "GEISHA", she began, "GEISHACANFURMAMANDANRAFAN".

But the young matron had not yet completed her shopping. She espied on a high shelf a small bowl which she decided to acquire for her pet bird's cage. The damsel behind the counter then disclosed that she had no head for heights and declined to climb up the stepladder to procure the small bowl. She demurred with the word ... "ADTUMMULAFF". The customer made the comment, "WUDJI?" and volunteered to hold the stepladder steady. She gave the undertaking, "ALHUDJI ALNONUDJI".

Still the damsel refused to mount the steps and bring down the bowl for the bird's cage. The housewife, her heart set on purchasing the bowl, issued the stern command, "WUDJI GERRATBOUL!"

The rely was an emphatic negative. At this juncture, I regret to say, the young housewife became extremely exasperated. But, despite her ire, she demonstrated the Glaswegian native's innate love of poetry in the lyrical rebuke she directed at the obstinate maiden who refused to provide her with the pet bird's bowl ... I listened entranced as she declaimed –

AHYADUDJI AHCANNIBUDJI
AHWANTITRATBOUL
FURMABUDJIZCLUDJI!

Upatraburd's

Lecturer: We illustrate this language lesson with a playlet in which we hear the native patois as it is spoken in a Glaswegian home. First of all we see a mother and father seated in the kitchen of their residence. They are silent until the doorbell rings.

Mother: Ratsa door! Whit ur ye sittin' therr in yur simmit fur? Pirroan yur jaickit!

Father: Eh?

Mother: Yur jaickit. It'll be Ella an hur fella.

Father: Aw, izzi aff his work?

Mother: He's took ra night aff.

THE FATHER STRUGGLES INTO HIS JACKET. THE MOTHER HURRIES TO OPEN THE FRONT DOOR. SHE RETURNS TO THE KITCHEN WITH HER DAUGHTER ELLA AND THE BOY FRIEND, SAMMY. THE YOUNG MAN IS CARRYING AN UMBRELLA.

Father: Aw Ella's fella lumburs hur hame wi' a numburella!

Sammy: (RESENTFULLY) Why ra hell should Ella's fella no' lumbur Ella wi' a numburella?

Ella: Ach gi'es ra gamp. (SHE SNATCHES THE UMBRELLA AND THROWS IT INTO A CORNER.

THEN SHE ADDRESSES HER PARENTS)Ur youse yins no' gaun' oot?

Mother: Naw ... Thur nae binga oan ra night.

Sammy: (ASIDE TO ELLA) Heh, you sayed if Ah came up here the night we'd be able tae ...

Ella: Shurrit. (TO PARENTS) Ur yiz no' gaun' ben the hoose tae watch ra telly?

Father: Naw ... Ra telly's broke.

Sammy: (HANDING THE FATHER A BANKNOTE) Away you wi' the wife an' huv a wee bevvy.

Mother: Oh, 'sa fiver!

Father: (TO SAMMY) Huv you stertit workin' over-time?

Sammy: Naw ... No' till you an' yur missus leaves the hoose.

Father: (TO MOTHER) Come oan, Cynthia. Doon tae ra pub.

THE PARENTS EXIT.

SAMMY IMMEDIATELY CLASPS ELLA TO HIM.

Ella: Lay aff, ya nyaff! Ma wee sister'll be here in a minnit!

Sammy: Yur wee sister nixt!! You sayed if Ah came up here the night we'd ...

Ella: Cley up ... Here she's noo.

GIRL ENTERS. SHE IS ATTRACTIVE AND WEARING A VERY SHORT SKIRT. SAMMY GAPES AT HER.

Sammy: So THIS is yur sister?

Sister: That's right ... Jist youse carry on. Ah'm gaun' tae ra disco ... But Ah'm gaun' ben tae the room first. Thur's a cake in therr an' Ah'm dyin' fur a slice o' it.

THE SISTER EXITS.

Ella: (COYLY) She's gaun oot! We'll huv the hoose tae wursel's!

SHE PUTS HER ARMS ROUND SAMMY'S NECK.

BUT HE DISENGAGES AND MAKES FOR THE
DOOR.

Ella: Ur ye gaun 'tae ra loo?

Sammy: Naw, ben tae ra room fur a slice o' cake.

Ella: Ya waster! Gaun' take a rinnin' jump tae yursel'!

Lecturer: Let us consider some of the more obscure words
and phrases we have heard in the drama enacted in the
home of the young lady, Ella. As the doorbell heralds the
approach of the lovers her mother reproaches her
husband with three scornful words ...

SITTIN ERRINYUR SIMMIT!

Clearly she is of the opinion that a simmit, or vest, is not
the correct dress for one who is about to receive a guest
in his home.

ERRINYUR

is freqently used by ladies when they are critical of their
husband's sartorial deficiences. So we have such
variations as ...

STAUNNIN ERRINYUR SHURT!
LYIN ERRINYUR GUIDSUIT!
FLOATINABOOT ERRINYUR BERRSPUDS!

And a fastidious matron who objects to her spouse's
unconventional night attire might be heard to declaim ...

SLEEPIN ERRINYUR COAMBIES!

The father in our play inquiries if his daughter's
gentleman friend is taking the evening off from his
employment. He asks...

IZZIAFFIZ WURK?

Note the word ...

IZZIAFFIZ

We use it as a prefix when seeking information. If we are
concerned about a male person's emaciated appear-
ance we pose the question ...

IZZIAFFIZ CHUCK?

Should we wish to determine whether or not he has

ceased to indulge in the immoderate consumption of alcohol, we ask...

IZZIAFFIZ BOOZIN?

If we become aware that a gentleman's behavioural pattern is tending towards the unorthodox then we say ...

IZZIAFFIZ RUDDIROACKUR?

More interesting words are heard when the lovers arrive at the house. The father derides his daughter's gentleman friend, or lumbur, for escorting her home with an umbrella. Spiritedly the gallant demands to know why he should not ...

LUMBUR ELLA WIA NUMBURELLA

You will notice that the letter "n" is added to the final word. So it appears as...

NUMBURELLA

A word beginning with the letter "n" is often preceded by ...

ZATNOA

A Glasgow native who treats with contumely a marital partner, politician or a television "personality" who rouses his or her ire is apt to exclaim ...

ZATNOA NASSIAFULLA?

And, of course, from one who receives an inflated gas or electricity bill or income tax demand there comes the familiar cry of despair ...

ZATNOA NOFFISEEKNUR?

Two other words denoting deep sorrow were spoken by the father and mother in the domestic drama. These were ...

**NAEBINGA-OANRANI' and
RATELLISBROKE**

Greatly heartened, they depart when the young man gives them the wherewithal to refresh themselves at a nearby hostelry. Their daughter Ella finds herself in the arms of her ardent wooer. He is not lacking in frankness as he makes the proposition ...

WHIRRABOORRA BASHATRAPASH?

The young lady appeals to him to moderate the intensity of his passion. She addresses him with the delightful rhyming word ...

LAYAFF-YANYAFF

In similar circumstances she could have made an even more emphatic request by using another rhyming word...

CURRITOOT-YADURTIBROOT

or, in an even greater emergency ...

NUFARATYARANDIRAT!

The lovers are again disturbed when the young sister appears on the scene. But she announces that she will adjourn to another apartment to partake of a slice of the cake she has purchased. Then she makes her tactful exit and Ella embraces the lumbur, Sammy. Suddenly he tears himseif from her arms and makes for the door. Anxiously she inquires ...

URYI GONTIRALOO?

She no doubt expected him to echo the word and reply ...

AYAM GONTIRALOO, TOORALOORANOO

But he did not utter these lovely words. Instead he stated that he was going to join her young sister and request her to give him a slice of her cake. With feminine intuition the maiden Ella concludes that the young man's primary desire is not for a piece of cake. And so, from the disillusioned damsel, we hear the age-old cry that has ended not a few Glasgovian romances ...

GONTAKKARINNINJUMPTIYURSEL!

Tips for Tourists

Lecturer: There are times when French, German, English and other foreign visitors to Glasgow have difficulty in understanding and being understood by some of the natives with whom they come in contact.

This lesson is designed to help non-Glaswegian friends to overcome certain linguistic impasses that might present themselves.

We commence with a sketch about a tourist from south of the border who is paying his first visit to the city. THE TOURIST IS IN A TAXI AND IN CONVERSATION WITH THE DRIVER.

Tourist: Drop me off at a decent restaurant

Driver: Ur ye furra tightnur?

Tourist: I want to have dinner.

Driver: Hud ye heehaw tae eat oan the train?

Tourist: They were not serving heehaw or any other dish. There was no dining-car

THE TAXI STOPS OUTSIDE A RESTAURANT

Driver: This is no' too bad a j'int.

Tourist: (LEAVING THE TAXI) What do I owe you?

Driver: Three quid.

Tourist: What? That's an exorbitant charge!

Driver: Rat's ra ferr.

THE TOURIST, SCOWLING, HANDS OVER THREE £1-NOTES AND STALKS OFF TOWARDS THE RESTAURANT. THE DRIVER CALLS AFTER HIM.

Driver: Heh, is thur heehaw tip?

THE TOURIST IGNORES HIM AND ENTERS THE RESTAURANT. AS HE TAKES HIS MEAL HE IS INTRIGUED BY THE CONVERSATION OF A YOUNG COUPLE AT A NEARBY TABLE.

Girl: Chuck us ower a bap, pal ... an' see'sa glessa ra rid biddy.

Man: Ah could dae wi' merr totties an' tumshie.

Girl: Ur you no' ferr stappit noo?

Man: Shut yur gub an' drink yur vino.

MYSTIFIED BY THIS EXCHANGE, THE TOURIST FINISHES HIS DINNER AND CALLS FOR THE BILL. HE IS SHOCKED AT THE LARGE AMOUNT HE IS BEING CHARGED.

Tourist: (TO WAITER) This is absolutely outrageous! £10 for a small fish and a few chips and a glass of wine that tastes like vinegar!

Waiter: Keep yur herr oan.

THE TOURIST FLINGS A £5-NOTE ON THE TABLE AND WALKS OFF.

Tourist: You're getting heehaw tenner out of ME!

Lecturer: It is small wonder that the tourist in our sketch is nonplussed by some of the native expressions he hears. Let us try to determine the significance of these. When he asks to be taken to a restaurant he is rather baffled by the taxidriver's question ...

URYEFURRA TYTNUR?

URYEFURRA

is more frequently used with the affix ...

HOF

This gives us the much-appreciated invitation ...

URYEFURRAHOF?
A gentleman who has accepted too many such invitations may express his dread at being confronted by his wife. He will then be asked the grave question ...

URYEFURRAHIJUMP
We next come to another inquiry from the taxi-driver that puzzled his passenger. He asks if, on the train from London, he had ...

HEEHAWTI EAT
Under the impression that the driver was referring to some sort of native dish, the tourist replies that no meal was served on the train, let alone ...

HEEHAWTI
The tourist complains that the £3 fare for the one-mile journey is far too much. Nevertheless he hands over the money. The taxi-driver is disappointed at not receiving the expected gratuity. Again he uses the word...

HEEHAWTI
He adds a single letter to convey his resentment. And so the word changes to ...

HEEHAWTIP!
Had the tourist been au fait with the Glasgow patois he could have censured the taxi-driver by exclaiming ...

YURRATTITMAC!
CUMMAFFITYU!
or
TAKMEFURRAMUGPAL?
In the restaurant the tourist is at a loss to understand the purport of the conversational exchange between the young lady and her gentleman friend at an adjacent table. She makes known her desire for an additional bread roll with the enchanting adjuration ...

CHUKKUZOURABAPAL
Next she expresses a wish for wine, using the traditional form of request ...

SEEZAGLESSARARIDBIDDI

Her escort seems a little distrait. He is anxious to obtain a second serving of the ancient Scottish delicacy ...

TOTTIZANTUMSHI

Suddenly the damsel realises that her dinner companion is proving to be too hearty a trencherman. Her concern on this score is demonstrated by her query...

URYUNO FERRSTAPPITNU?

The young gentleman ignores her warning. He invites her to perform the remarkable feat of imbibing wine with her mouth closed. He makes the suggestion ...

SHUTYURGUB ANDRINKUPYURVINO

Meanwhile the tourist has finished his dinner and asks for his bill. He makes a violent protest at the amount he is being charged. The waiter deals with the situation by intoning ...

KEEPYUR HERROAN

By this he means that the gentleman should preserve his equanimity.

KEEPYUR

is a key word in the Glasgois vocabulary. An appeal for calm is also effected in the advice ...

KEEP YURHEID

or more pedantically ...

RETAINRACRANIUM

The meaning of the word change subtly when a lady counsels her young daughter about the pitfalls that may await her when she goes out into the world. The mother will then use ...

KEEPYUR

with the addition of the word ...

HONOANYURHAPNI

and so we have the stern maternal warning ...

KEEPYUR HONOANYURHAPNI

As our sketch ends we see the infuriated tourist refusing to pay the £10 bill. As he throws a £5-note on the table and hurries from the restaurant he improvises on a

native word he has learned and informs the waiter that he will receive ...
HEEHAWTENNER!

The Professor

One Enchanted Evening

Before commencing my sociological research in Glasgow and its environs I had been informed by a learned friend that to spend a Sunday evening in that jewel of a city was a unique experience that stamped itself indelibly upon the memory. "There is," declared my friend, "nothing like it in the rest of the world."

Accordingly I wasted no time in savouring the Sunday evening delights of the great metropolis.

What an ambience of gaiety prevailed as I joined the throng of merrymakers who paraded the pavements which sparkled under a deluge of soft West of Scotland rain. Not a few of the promenaders spoke in a foreign tongue.

One lady revealed that the influence of the old Franco-Scottish Alliance was still extant. After a particularly heavy shower of rain she drew her husband's attention to her wet outer garment. Speaking in French, she asked him ...

DIEU SI MA CÔTÉ?

or, to give it its Glaswegian spelling ...

DYESEEMA COATEH?

Her husband pointed out that his coat, too, was far from dry. To my astonishment he elected to use the German language. He began his reply with ...

ACH MEIN GOTT

Then he added a word in what I took to be the Bavarian

vernacular ...

BLIDDISOAKTHRÜ

So that his statement in full was ...

ACH MEIN GOTT BLIDDISOAKTHRU

Happily most of the Sunday evening revellers preferred to converse in the lovely liquid accents of their native habitat. One youthful couple were partaking of an al fresco repast of fish and pommes frites. These they carried in paper bags. From the young lady came the observation ...

SNOMUCHIA

to which she added the attractive words ...

SUPPURFUR RAMUNNI.

Her gentleman friend appeared to concur with her verdict on the meal and proclaimed ...

SADAMPTSWINNUL!

Then impulsively he paid the damsel a graceful compliment, likening her to a Greek goddess ...

YURDIALZAWGREECE

She in turn praised the beauty of his visage, telling him ...

ALIKEYURBLOOMINCHEEK

And she bade him regard the reflection of his handsome countenance in a looking-glass with the charming suggestion ...

TAKKADEKKATYUR AINDAMPAN

It was not long ere I realised that it was trysting-time for lovers. One young swain braved the downpour as he waited his lovely young inamorata. When she arrived he was hailed with a fervent cry of ...

AH, LOVE!

But it seemed to me that there was a soupçon of irony in his tone when he appended the word ...

GETTINDROONDIT

and his greeting took the form of ...

ALLUV GETTINDROONDIT

But it was obvious to me that her cavalier, or lumbur, was prepared to overlook the late arrival of the damsel. What tenderness there was in his voice as he paid tribute to her with a quotation from a moving Gaelic love-poem ...

AYEYURTHERR
SJISTNUTTFERR
MACLAEZIZSOAKIN
ANYIDONTGIADOACKIN

Overcome by emotion, the young lady then addresed her amour by his full and impressive cognomen, crying.

MONTY! MONTY!
MONTY HELLOOTAHERE!

It was something of a revelation to me when I observed that many of the natives were patrons of the cinema. As they approach a film theatre their custom is to stop suddenly and give vent to the ritual chant ...

THURRACUE! THURRACUE! THURRACUE A MILELONG!

I was saddened by the sight of one elderly gentleman who passed me. He, it would seem, nurtured a hopeless passion for a screen idol of yesteryear. There was nostalgia in his voice as he called her name ...

AVA! OH, AVA!

and he went on to express his devotion to her in the old Gallowgatean dialect ...

AVA! AVAHELLAVA THURSTOANMI!

As the jolly Sunday evening wore on, the happy throng, splashing merrily through the rain, was augmented by a strange and picturesque band of young natives, male and female. They wore shorts and bore on their backs heavy burdens from which hung pots, kettles, guitars and sundry other articles. I concluded that they were itinerant merchants from the remote trading post known as Rabarras.

I smiled upon one of the young females of the tribe and offered to purchase one of the antique cooking utensils suspended from her pack. To my delight she not only spoke English but intimated that she would make me a present of one of her wares. "I'll give you this pot," she told me.

Then, lapsing into the obscure argot of Rabarras, she

continued ...
ALGIEYIT OWERYUR BALDIOLCRUST
What a delightful end to an evening of enchantment!

Broadcasting Techniques

Lecturer: I would like, if I may, to draw your attention to some of the words and phrases we hear, perhaps too frequently, from radio and television broadcasters. I trust that these ladies and gentlemen may draw some slight benefit from the theories I am about to propound.

It is a matter for regret that they rarely if ever, make use of the beautiful language spoken by many of their Scottish listeners.

One of the oft-repeated sayings heard over the air is "Thank you very much indeed". This is directed at persons who have given interviews. Perhaps could be replaced by such Glaswegian expressions of gratitude as ...

THANXALOT
FERRANUFFMAC

or even

TAPAL

All too often in television plays a lady or gentleman will make an exit with the intimation, "I'll see myself out". I suggest that this might be changed, in Scottish plays at least, to ...

AMFURRAFF
ALFINDRADOORMASEL

or the more specific

DONTGERRUP, CHEERIBYRANOO

In dramatic works emanating from the United States characters frequently pose the brusque question, "What are you talking about?" Desirable variants are...

WHISSATYUSAYED?
WHIDDYEMEAN?
WHITTURYEGERRINAT?

Greatly do I admire the solicitude shown to the victims of untoward occurrences in television dramas. A lady or gentleman knocked to the ground by a malefactor, hurled from a blazing motorcar, thrown from a high building or otherwise rendered hors de combat will, as often as not, find a person bending over them and inquiring anxiously, "Are you all right?"

I submit that it might be more true to life if they employed the traditional Glaswegian expressions of concern ...

HOOHUTYI?
HOOGIEDYIRAKEEKUR?
JIWAANTA CUPLASPRIN?

or the even more compassionate

GETRASOWLABRANDY

You may have noticed that the players in American television dramas are peculiarly addicted to the pleasures of the table. A gentleman will lure a prepossessing damsel into his company by inviting her to accompany him to a "li'l Mexican place downtown where we kin gedda marvullus chili con carne". Almost invariably the young lady exclaims, "Yeah, Ah sure wud like that." Were she a Glasgow maiden she would be accustomed to a much greater variety in the forms of invitations to dine out. Such as ...

MOANFURRACOAFFY
ALSTONYIA BAGGACHIPS
FANCIATYTNUR?

And the seal has been set on many a romantic liaison

with the tender query ...

COODJI GOAPIE?

One television expert who explains to us the intricacies of football is wont to proclaim, "That's a good-looking ball!" He is not, of course, referring to the agreeable rotundity of the leathern sphere but to the accuracy with which one player has propelled it to a colleague on the field. I suggest that the expert might vary his encomium with such attractive Glaswegianisms as ...

THASSARERRBAW!

RATPASSIZMAAAAAGIC!

IZPITTITAERAFITTOKENNY!

Let us consider now the weather forecasts. Interest in these would be heightened if they were couched in these vivid meteorological terms ...

SGONNICUMDOON CATSANDUGZ CERRIABROL-LIRAMORRA

MERRSNAW, PIRROANYURWELLIZ

and warning us of low temperatures in prospect ...

KEEPOANYURCOAMBIZ

and

NORAWERRUR FURBRASSMUNGKIZ

I am most grateful to you for giving me your attention. Thank you very much indeed ... er ...

AWCHINAS THANXAMILLYUN.

The Professor

In the Park

What a treasure trove of linguistic gems I lighted upon when my study of Glaswegianology took me to one of the great city's public parks! I found it full of happy citizens, male and female of all ages. Soon I was taking copious notes of the beautiful words and phrases that fell from their lips.

But I must confess to some apprehension when I heard a matron menacing her small offspring with a peculiar form of chastisement. It appeared that he had reiterated a strong desire for ice-cream and she threatened him with ...

ALPOKEYHATYE!

Then, to a lady who accompanied her, she made an astounding statement about her diminutive son. I translated it as meaning that he was a crimson sea bird. She declared ...

RATWEANZA RUDDIGANNET

Next she put forward the incredible claim that he was aided in his consumption of ice cream by an orchestral accompaniment. She contended that he could eat it ...

TIABAUNPLAYN

I waited in the hope of seeing the infant virtuoso perform his masticatory feat. But his mother refused to purchase more ice-cream. She did, however, promise him what I imagined was a Scottish delicacy ...

ASCUDOANRALUG

Leaving the happy family, I made my way into the rustic

recesses of the park. There I encountered two maidens in swimming attire who were lying at their ease on the greensward. My curiosity was aroused when one of them, a comely redhead, revealed to a passing acquaintance that they were waiting for ...

RASSUNTI

Was this, I asked myself, the name of a religious leader revered by the natives and about to pay them a pastoral visit? But I rejected this theory when the maiden called out ...

KUMMOOT

After some concentration I came to the conclusion that the young ladies wished to acquire a tan and were waiting for ...

RASSUNTI KUMMOOT

I was congratulating myself on determining the meaning of the phrase when I perceived two young gentlemen who were surveying with interest the recumbent females. One of the gallants remarked to his friend, Noah ...

NOAH BADPERRABURDS

The other addressed his friend as "Ivan" ...

IVAN EYEFURRARIDHEID

Eventually the two young ladies became aware of their admirers' presence. The badinage that ensued illustrated the remarkable linguistic versatility of the great city's inhabitants. The red-haired Glaswegienne called to the young males in Russian ...

AWSKI DADDLE ... BUGGRAFF!

Her admirer, Ivan, at once hailed her by her exotic Russian name ...

GITNOATTITYA NASTIBITCH

As I am not versed in any of the Slavonic languages, I left the quartet to their exchange of pleasantries and bent my steps towards a large lake. Many Clydesiders, with their traditional love of maritime pursuits, were braving the watery element in small craft known as

OARIBOATS

It was heartening to see how assiduously the heads of

families taught their progeny the intricacies of seamanship. One juvenile who proposed to take his parents on a voyage over the lake was not fully conversant with the technique of rowing. His father at once issued the nautical command ...

YURERSS TAERASHERPEND!

Alas, the oarsman stood up to change his position on the seat and caused the craft to turn over. He and his parents were precipitated into the water and were obliged to wade ashore. Crestfallen over his error, the embryo mariner ran off. His father hurried after him, promising to give him further navigational instruction. In his distinctive patois he assured him ...

ALLERNYI TICOWPRABOAAAT

As I made my way towards the park exit I passed the red-haired young lady and her companion. They now lay upon their backs in the sunshine. I ventured to address them in their own language with ...

RASSUNZOOTNOO!

The red-haired damsel immediateiy sat upright and regarded me with an interest I found quite flattering. All at once, in the lilting language of the Gael, she trilled ...

ALPITMA

adding a word to it to complete what I had no doubt was an ancient Hebridean blessing ...

ALPITMA FITUPYURJAXI!

The IT People

Lecturer: A language most non-Glaswegians find rather difficult to understand is that spoken by certain inhabitants who, in their discourse, feature the syllable"IT".

We illustrate this in a playlet in which we see two of the IT people, Margrit and Dauvit, attending a charity bazaar.

Dauvit: Whit is it, Margrit?

Margrit: Sajumble, Dauvit. Let's tak a dek at it. Ah don't fancy it.

Margrit: Aw, stoap moanin' aboot it! C'moan inty it ... Here a stall wi' claes fur sale oan it.

Dauvit: Ach Ah see it.

Margrit: Erra rerr checkit jaickit oan it, Dauvit. Whit aboot it?

Dauvit: Whit aboot whit?

Margrit: Aw, ye're real glaikit. Ra nice checkit jaickit! It's smart, intit?

Dauvit: Ah'd reyther go nakit than werr that dampt jaickit!

Margrit: Try it. Pit it oan.

   DAUVIT GIVES IN AND PUTS ON THE JACKET.

Dauvit: It's not bad, intit no'?

Margrit: Whit a rerr fit, Dauvit!

THE WOMAN IN CHARGE OF THE STALL APPEARS

Dauvit: (TO WOMAN) Whidd'ye waant fur it?

Woman: Waant fur whit?

Dauvit: This checkit jaickit.

Woman: Aw, it? A fifty-pee bit an' ye can huv it.

A BURLY MAN IN HIS SHIRT SLEEVES RUNS UP TO THE STALL AND ANGRILY ADDRESSES DAUVIT.

Man: Dammit, that's ma jaickit! Gi'e's it!

Woman: Ah sell't it.

Man: You should get yur heid feltit.

Margrit: Aff wi' it, Dauvit! Gi'e him it afore ye get beltit.

Lecturer: The regrettable contretemps at the clothing stall provides us with some typical speech patterns of the IT-speakers. The young man, Dauvit, is not sure about what is taking place in the hall. He queries his sweetheart with a word often used in the language ...

WHITIZZIT?

Other kindred words are ...

WHERRIZZIT?

and the more obscure ...

WHYRAHELLIZZIT?

which is used by a female of the IT tribe when she disapproves of her husband's inability to cope with a surfeit of liquid refreshments. To it she appends a second word, and so we have the pertinent question ...

WHYRAHELLIZZIT YUTAKKITWHENYICANNIHOD-DIT?

In our playlet the young lady, Margrit, explains to her escort, or "intendit", as he is termed, what is taking place in the hall. She utters the non-IT word ...

SAJUMMUL

But she reverts to her native IT tongue with the suggestion that they ...

TAKKADEKKATIT

When Dauvit indicates that he does not wish to visit the bazaar she makes what appears to be two contradictory statements. First she requests him to cease grumbling ...

STOAPMOANIN ABOOTIT

Then, with feminine fickleness, she invites him to resume complaining ...

MOAN INTYIT

The damsel is, in fact, instructing him to accompany her into the hall. And there she points out to her intendit what she considers to be a modish article of male attire. The beauty of the IT language is heard in her enthusiastic call ...

ERRARERRCHECKITJAICKITDAUVIT!

To this she appends the native word ...

WHIRRABOOTIT?

He quickly ripostes with ...

WHIRRABOOTWHIT?

With loving patience Margrit once more draws his attention to the checked garment. In so doing she breaks into a charming rhyme ...

AWYURREALGLAIKIT
RANICECHECKITJAICKIT

She urges him to try on the jacket. But he demurs with an equally appealing stave ...

ADREYTHERGONAKIT
THANWERRTHATDAMPTJAICKIT

But eventually he puts it on and his fair companion signifies her approbation with the lilting IT-word ...

WHITTARERRFITDAUVIT!

At this juncture the lady in charge of the stall appears and after brisk financial negotiations she intimates to Dauvit in the IT tongue ...

AFIFTIPEEBIT ANYIKINHUVVIT

But a grievous misunderstanding has occurred. The checked jacket is not for sale. It belongs to a large gentleman who, feeling the heat, had placed it on the clothing stall while he had gone off to see a Mr James Riddell. Naturally he is considerably taken aback when he sees that a stranger is wearing it. He makes a stentorian protest ...

DAMMITRATSMAJAICKIT! GIESIT!

He is further incensed when the lady in charge of the stall reveals her transaction ...

ASELTIT

The large man then questions the lady's sanity and proposes that she should seek medical attention, advising her...

GETYURHEIDFELTIT

But now Margrit senses that danger is imminent and urges her lumbur to restore the jacket to its infuriated owner. Again the enchanting cadences of the IT language delights our ears as she warns ...

AFFWITDAUVIT
GIEITHIMAFOREYEGITBELTIT.

If I may use a word in that most difficult language ...

GOADAHOPEYIZGERRIT.

The Professor joins a Migration

From a reliable source I learned that, during the summer months, many Glaswegians forsake their native habitat and migrate to Spain. It is obvious to me that they do this in order to broaden their outlook and make themselves better acquainted with the life-style of those who are not fortunate enough to reside in the captivating city on the Clyde.

So I resolved to take part in the great international trek of these avid seekers after knowledge. I joined a band of these academic adventurers at the city's airport. You can imagine how impressed I was when I heard many of them using Spanish words and phrases. As we entered the aircraft one lady said excitedly to her husband ...

AMFIERTO
AMFIERTO FLYINBOAB!

The gentleman commented with an affectionate ...

AMIGO!
AMIGONNI HUVTI SUFFURRIS?

As the aircraft rose so also did the spirits of my fellow-passengers. One Spanish-speaking migrant looked down at the clouds which hung over his native city and remarked ...

SIERRA

And he went on to explain to me ...

SIERRA GLESCAFERRWERRA

It did my heart good to see the carefree camaraderie that

prevailed as the flight to Spain continued. My fellow-travellers refreshed themselves with the traditional vacation potation ...

JOOTIFREE

One celebrant held out his bottle to me with the warm invitation ...

MAÑANA

quickly incorporating the Spanish word into his own language ...

MANYANEEDAGIDDRAM

Great was the euphoria when we arrived at our destination. The warm Mediterranean air was filled with the joyous exclamations ...

RATRIPWIZTOARTCHUR

JINGZAMJIGGURT

and

WHERZRALAVVI?

A buxom matron gave vent to her delight at being on Spanish soil with what I felt sure was an ancient Caledonian victory cry ...

MABAHOOKISERRWISITTIN

But later I heard a lady express disapproval of the scaffolding that covered the walls of the half-built hotel into which she and her husband had been booked. Loudly she uttered the Spanish word ...

ARRIBA!

She too adapted the word to her own native tongue as she informed her husband ...

ARRIBAMPOATS SWINULTUS!

I was given to understand that she was referring to the travel agent who had arranged her holiday and that she intended to complain to someone. In fact she made skilful use of the Spanish for "to compiain" ...

QUEJARSE

She replaced the first syllable "QUEJ" with the sinister Glaswegian term ...

KIKOANRA

But the great majority of the migrant Glaswegians pursued their sociological studies with the utmost assiduity, quickly becoming proficient in the local language. Outside a dress shop I heard one maiden declare ...

RATPONCHO COSTA MINTAMUNNI

A pale-faced gentleman, after partaking of a seafood dinner, favoured the Catalan dialect ...

OGOADMA KYTES GIENMIJIP!

And a lady whose husband, after visiting a bodega, lay on the sun-drenched beach, spoke of him in the local patois. She observed to a friend ...

ESPANOL ...
ESPANOL GITAZRIDZA BLIDDIFIRE

Ah, what gifted linguists are those intellectuals who make up the population of that glamorous metropolis in the West!

The Professor makes a
Gastronomic Discovery

A momentous discovery during my research into the Glaswegian language came when, on a visit to Paris, I entered a modest restaurant called Chez les Bachles. I found listed on its bill of fare a dish which bore the exotic title "Dumpline en Clute Ecossaise". The portion I ordered was truly delicious and I requested that my compliments be conveyed to the chef.

Judge of my astonishment when the creator of the delectable dish proved to be a Scottish lady, the spouse of the establishment's proprietor. She addressed me in her native language ...

"AWYIGOFUR RACLOOTIDUMPLIN?"

I begged her to let me have the recipe. With true Glaswegian graciousness she dictated to me the instructions on how to make that culinary masterpiece ...

DUMPLINE EN CLÛTÉ ÉCOSSAISE

As long as ye keep the heid it's nae boather makin' a clootie dumplin'. First of a', gether thegither a ferr-sized basin, a big boul, a big poat, a plate that'll fit inty the poat, aboot a squerr yerd o' cotton cloath an' a dauda string. An' a kettle oan the bile.

Here's whit goes inty the dumplin' ...

punna self-raisin' floour,

punna currants an' a haunfa o' raisins,
quartera punna suet,
haufa punna granulatit sugar,
fower wee teaspoonsfa o' mixed spice,
a big pincha saut,
some mulk.

Rummle up the hale jing-bang in the boul, addin' a wee tate mulk so's ye get a dough that's stiff an' no' runny. Tim some bilin' watter oot the kettle inty the fit o' the basin an' spread the cloath (or cloot) oan tap o' the watter.

Cowp the hale o' yur dough oot the boul an' oan tae the cloot in the basin. Draw the coarnurs o' the cloot the gither an' tie wi' the string.

Don't tie the string too tight or the dumplin' might burst efter swellin' up an' ye'll be in a helluva mess.

Noo ye've a big bag o' dough aboot the size o' a fitba'. Nixt ye pit a plate in the fit o' the big poat. Then gently ye lower the dumplin' oan tae the plate. Efter that poor as much bilin' watter inty the poat as will cover yur dumplin'.

Efter a' this cairry-oan ye'll mibbe waant a cuppa tea an a fag or even a wee lie-doon. Anyway, whitivvur ye dae, don't let the dumplin' simmer fur mair than three-an'-a-hauf oors. Efter that time wheech it oot the poat an' oan tae a plate. Peel aff the cloot an' therr ye huv a dish fit tae set afore a dizzen Egon Thingmys.

Mr Ballhead, Ballet Dancer

Mr Bailhead is a character I've got myself into over the years on radio and television. He is a self-confident Glaswegian who holds forth with great eloquence to anyone who will listen to him. He enunciates carefully and has a fine Scottish contempt for English words and grammar.

In the following television interview he is seen in his role of Serge Jaickitoff, ballet dancer.

> Scene: A dance studio.
> Cast: SERGE JAICKITOFF.
>   MAISIE VISCOUNT, Television interviewer.
>
> SERGE IS SEEN WHIRLING ROUND THE STUDIO, PROGRESSIVE FOUETTES IN-CREASING TO A VERY FAST RATE.
> Maisie: The man you are now watching is one of the world's most remarkable dancers. He is an incomparable artist, a premier danseur of great renown, a man who has devoted his life to the ballet. He is ... Serge Jaickitoff.
> CLOSE-UP OF DANCER AT PRACTICE BAR.
> Serge: How are ye? ... I was just having a small rummle-up before I get tore into Lez Silfyides this evening.
> Maisie: Mr Jaickitoff, I believe that, despite your

name, you are of Scottish descent.

Serge: (TAKING CIGARETTE STUB FROM BEHIND HIS EAR AND LIGHTING UP) That is correct. I made my descent on the world in the pretty little Renfrewshire village of Nitshill.

Maisie: And the name ... "Serge Jaickitoff"?

Serge: Well, I may as well reveal to you that that is an assumed name, or nom dee dance, as we say. I decided for to use this cognomium after confabulations with my friend Nureyev. Him and I decided that Serge Jaickitoff sounded much more glamorouser than John Ballhead.

Maisie: I see ... You mentioned Nureyev.

Serge: Yes. Ackchally he was the gent that discovered me. He was the first to realise that, as a ballet dancer, I was a natcheral.

Maisie: How did that come about, Mr Jaickitoff?

Serge: Quite fortuatatiously. To let you understand, I was always noted for my louping propensities. I was what could be termed a congential louper. Of course, my farra assisted me to develop this unusual gift. Often he would give me what he called in his quaint Scottish way a scud on the gub. Consequentially I was louping from early infanticide right up to the age of adultery.

Maisie: And how did you come to meet Nureyev?

Serge: Eh? ... Oh, big Rudy? Weil, it happened in a very extraneous way. He was in Glasgow at the time and he was walking along Great Western Road when, all of a sudden, he observed a most unusual sight. It was none urra than myself. I was in the act of louping on to the hin'-end of a scaffy wagon. That was then my vacation. "Bravo!" yelled Nureyev, "Bravo!" Then he came over and congratulated me. "Never," he said, "have I saw such perfect louping!" He talked impregnable English. Thereupon, without no further ado, we discussed my natcheral ineptitude for the ballet. Nureyev gave me the most unvaluable advice. "Huv a bash," he said. That very day I resigned from the cleansing department and soon I was on my way to London to join the corpse.

Maisie: What do you mean exactly ... the corpse?

Serge: The Corpse dee Ballet. Before you could say "Paddy Do" I became dediacatit to the terpsechorian art ... Got a fag on ye? ... Ta.

    TAKES CIGARETTE FROM MAISIE, LIGHTS IT, INHALES DEEPLY AND COUGHS.

    It must be the dust off that floor.

Maisie: A male dancer, of course, must keep very fit.

Serge: Aw, definately. To we exponuents of the ballet physical fitness is of paranoid importance. To let you understand, considerable feats of strength is called upon when we come in contract with certain ballerynas and other impedimentia of the ballet. For instance, one has to be veritable Colosseum of strength when dancing with the celebratit Svetlana Bulginova.

Maisie: Why is that?

Serge: Well, you see, this large dansooze – often referred to as the Jumbo jet of the ballet world – is no lightweight. In addition, before she goes on the stage to embark on her balletical pererigrinations she is very partial to a couple of pies with a pint or two of heavy. Hence, you can imagine that the burling round of this gargantuacious lady calls for more than a moducum of endeavour. Oh yes ... Well do I remember setting her in motion during our performance of The Nutcracker Suit. So great was the velocity of those giant revolving haughs that I was propagatit across the stage with the most utmostest force. Before I could stop myself I hit the Sugar Plum Fairy a severe dunt right in the middle of her arabesque.

Maisie: How unfortunate ... I notice, Mr Jaickitoff, that you seem to smoke quite a lot. How many cigarettes do you smoke a day?

Serge: Aw, not more than eighty ... Mind you, sometimes I've got to borrow another twinty from big Svetlana.

Maisie: I see ... Well, I understand you're coming along to our studio here tomorrow for a recording of your new ballet, "La Tristesse d'un Petit Nyaff", which viewers will see in the evening.

Serge: That is correct.

Maisie: Good! We'll look forward to seeing you at 10.30 tomorrow morning.

Serge: Oh hivvins, no' ten-thirty in the mornin'!

Maisie: Why not?

Serge: Ah don't stoap coughin' till two!

Mr Ballhead as
The Marathon Runner

Marathon running is one of Mr Ballhead's many activities. Interviewed on television by Maisie Viscount, he gives a modest account of how he achieved fame in that port.

Maisie: To John Ballhead the winning of marathons is one of the most important things in his busy life ... Mr Ballhead, you are always running .

Ballhead: Aye, Ah'm always runnin' oota fags. Have ye got one on ye?

MAISIE GIVES HIM A CIGARETTE AND LIGHTS IT FOR HIM

Ta! ... Aw that's better. Nuthin' like a fag for gettin' yur braith back.

Maisie: You are known as the Master of the Marathon.

Ballhead: That is so. Of course, my chinas call me "Shelfheid".

Maisie: "Shelfheid"! That's a strange name!

Ballhead: Yes ... Ackchally this unusual nom dee plum emanuates from the shape of my head. You may have noticed it sticks out at the back in no unseemly manner.

Maisie: Yes it does rather.

Ballhead: Well, I may tell you that this streamlined cranium of mines is at the foot of my success as a marathon runner.

Maisie: Oh, is it? Am I to take it that the specially light weight of your head gives you an advantage over other runners?

Ballhead: No, no. It's a matter of airio dynamics. To let you understand – when I am running in a marathon the projecting portion of my skull cuts the wind resistance to a minewmum. Hence, at the rear of my napper a tempurry vackyum is created. Now the air rushes into this vackyum at such a dinger that my cranium is shoved forward with great acceleration ... Of course, to keep up with it my feet have tae go like the ruddy clappers.

Maisie: That's remarkable ... How did your running career start?

Ballhead: Well, my proclivity for high-speed perambulating did not manifestate itself until I reached the age of indiscretion. It was then that I became deeply inflatulated with a young lady.

Maisie: Ah, she encouraged you in your ambition?

Ballhead: She certingly did! The minute I suggested taking her into the woods to study nature she agreed. Without no further ado I grabbed her by the hand and we set off. Such was the velocity of my running that the young lady was rendered completely breathless.

Maisie: Weren't you breathless too?

Ballhead: Yes ... but not until we came out of the woods. Thereafter we made a number of high-speed visitations to these sylvan glades. Spurred on by love, I went faster and faster. I then became aware that I possessed this gargantuacious gift of running.

Maisie: I see ... And how do you relax?

Ballhead: Aw I usually indulge in jay-jogging.

Maisie: JAY-jogging?

Ballhead: Precisely ... Many a happy hour I spend amongst the traffic in Sauchiehall Street. You see, in many cities people are fined and otherwise inhibitated from enjoying themselves on busy thoroughfares. But Glasgow is more broader-minded towards pedestrians. As a result our freedom-loving city has became the Mecca for jay-joggers from all over the civilised world, and also from London.

Maisie: I didn't realise that.

Ballhead: Oh yes ... It may interest you to know that in 1985 Glasgow will be the venue for the Olympic Jay-Jogging Championships. I myself will be taking part in the two main events.

Maisie: Oh ... and what are these events?

Ballhead: Well, there's the 1,500 metres Handicap Race in which the competitors jog across the street in front of two buses while perusing a copy of Playboy or some other instructive volume. Then there is the High Jump for the coveted Jay-Jogging Heidcase Cup. This simply entails getting out of a taxi on the wrong side and louping in front of a sports car driven by an inebriated short-sighted gent.

Maisie: It all sounds rather hazardous.

Ballhead: Ah but you don't think of the dangers when your ambition is to be the Sebastian Coe of the jay-jogging world.

Maisie: I see ... Well, thank you very much indeed, John Ballhead. I won't keep you any longer from your training.

Ballhead: That's all right. I've already did my daily half-hour. I'm away home for a tightnur.

Maisie: A meal? Well, bon appetit!

Ballhead: No, a HIGH tea ... Is ma taxi there?

Maisie: You're taking a TAXI? But your home's only a 100 yards from here!

Ballhead: I know, hen ... But I hate walkin'. It tires me oot.

The Dog called 'Parliamo Glasgow'

It was to be the first time a Parliamo Glasgow sketch would be seen on an Edinburgh stage and Stanley feared the pantomime audiences at the King's Theatre wouldn't understand it. But they did and it wasn't a flop. By way of celebrating Stanley dashed out to Corstorphine, bought a young pedigree boxer dog from a noted breeder there and gave it to me as a Christmas present. I wrapped the little animal in my overcoat and took him home to Glasgow by train.

Stanley suggested the boxer should be called "Parliamo Glasgow" and the pup was registered at the Kennel Club under that name.

Parli, as he came to be called, grew into a big powerful chap, a splendid specimen of his breed. He looked fierce but was the sweetest-natured of dogs and he was immensely popular with all who met him.

Appropriately enough, he quickly became au fait with various Glaswegianisms. Expressions that delighted him came from the young ladies serving in shops. His tail wagged in ecstasy when he heard ...

AVABISKITFORPARLI

or

WANNAWEEBITLIVERPET?

But he seemed hurt when an anxious mother would bid her offspring ...

KEEPAWAFAERATDUG!

with the quite unnecessary warning ...

ITLTAKRAHAUNAFFYE!

But, reassured that Parli adored children, the mother would say admiringly ...

ZANOFFINICEBIGDUG

or, proudly, ...

RAWEANZNO FEARTFURRIM

All too frequently our canine heart-throb was offered titbits and great was his joy when he heard such questions as ...

JIWAANTACHIPSON?

WULLAGIEMA WEEDAUDAMAPIE?

and

DIZZILIKESMARTIES?

Young suburban damsels seemed fascinated by his big brown eyes. He seemed to enjoy being fussed over by them as they gave vent to such eulogies as ...

OHMAI HESGAWRJUSS!

and ...

HEEZAREELLILAHVLIBOY!

A Kelvinside matron who visited us was surprised to see Parli sleeping back-to-back with the cat in front of the fire. He looked up perplexed when she cried out poetically ...

FENCITHET!
BECKTOBECK
WITH YOUR
BIGBLECKCET!

Parli's popularity grew with the years and Glaswegian generosity saw increased offers to him of steak, sole, pies, sweets, cakes, biscuits and even, on one occasion, a soupçon of smoked salmon.

My daughter, a dog expert, had a hard struggle keeping Parliamo Glasgow, the boxer, from becoming the fattest dog in Scotland.   *ALEX MITCHELL*

The Pedigree Certificate for 'Parliamo Glasgow' – a splendid specimen of his breed.

Also available from

BIRLINN

PARA HANDY

Collected stories from *The Vital Spark*,
In Highland Harbours with Para Handy &
Hurricane Jack of the Vital Spark

Neil Munro

Introduced by *Brian Osborne* and *Ronald Armstrong*

This, first ever complete Para Handy, contains all the stories
from Neil Munro's previous collections, plus fifteen entirely
new stories, discovered this year. The new stories show Munro
writing at the height of his powers about Para Handy and the
Great War, Para Handy and the Naval Review of 1912, and
Para Handy and the introduction of radio in Scotland.

Brian Osborne and Ronnie Armstrong provide a full
introduction and notes to each of the stories, rendering this the
definitive 'Para Handy'.

ISBN 1 874744 02 5

WILLIAM McGONAGALL

Collected Poems

'The most startling incident in my life was the time I discovered myself to be a poet, which was in the year 1877'

Since then thousands of people the world over have enjoyed the verse of Scotland's alternative national poet - William McGonagall. This omnibus edition brings together in one volume the three famous collections *Poetic Gems*, *More Poetic Gems* and *Last Poetic Gems* and includes all the valuable autobiographical material which appeared in the original volumes. It includes all his most famous work 'The Tay Bridge Disaster', 'The Death of Lord and Lady Dalhousie', and many more.

ISBN 1 874744 01 7